Competing for Global Dominance

Survival in a Changing World

By Jack S. Katz

Foreword by Bob Karr
CEO, LinkSV

E-mail: info@superstarpress.com
20660 Stevens Creek Blvd., Suite 210
Cupertino, CA 95014

First Printing: July 2010
Paperback ISBN: 978-1-60773-042-2 (1-60773-042-1)
eBook ISBN: 978-1-60773-043-9 (1-60773-043-X)
Place of Publication: Silicon Valley, California, USA
Paperback Library of Congress Number: 2010929457

Trademarks

Warning and Disclaimer

"This critical assessment of international business practices unlocks the paradigms of our global economy and the significance for global partnerships to succeed in our ever changing twenty-first century economy."
Tony Marienthal, Chairman European Union ISDN User Forum Users Workshop, Official Auditor European Union Research in Advanced Communications for Europe, European Union Negotiator General Agreement on Tariffs and Trade (GATT) Uruguay Round /Maastricht Treaty

"Jack Katz presents a comprehensive guide for businesses that are either contemplating entering the U.S. market or have already begun the process. In his book he lays out the foundational legal, cultural, and financial strategies for success. Too often foreign businesses do not appreciate how much time and money can be lost without a comprehensive guide like this showing them the way. I highly recommend this book to my clients—both domestic and international."
Michael Moradzadeh Esq., Rimon Law Group

Dedication

To Caren, for all her love, support, and enthusiasm in making this book possible.

Acknowledgments

If I have learned anything from writing *Competing for Global Dominance* it's that I could not have done it alone. The ideas that are molded together here were bandied about and refined by many extraordinarily insightful colleagues and friends.

The initial concept and inspiration for this book occurred during discussions with my colleagues during the time I was employed at Sun Microsystems and Cisco Systems. We all became aware of many of the problems that faced both foreign and domestic companies when they tried to enter new global markets with their products and services. The issues were just beginning to emerge as we explored along with our worldwide partners ways to better understand these business conditions and then to solve them.

I would like to thank Bodo Parody, Ph.D., for without his guidance the book would not be so encompassing; Bob Karr, networker extraordinaire, for his foresight on the dynamics of Silicon Valley and his exuberance; Alexander von Gimbut, for our conversations on the effects of globalization and trade; Aviad Kamara, for his knowledge, foresight and leadership in bringing business opportunities together; and Larry Hausen, who has the eye to move people with his images, design, and style.

I am grateful to the numerous foreign trade commissioners, consuls general, ambassadors, and directors of various chambers of commerce that I have worked with over the years. I would especially like to thank for their friendship and input: Shai Aizin, Consul for Economic Affairs, Government of Israel Economic Mission; Marianne Toftegaard Poulssen, former Director, Innovation Center Denmark–Silicon Valley; Frederic Delbart, Trade and Investment Commissioner, Belgian Trade Commission; Christian Kuegerl, Austrian Trade Commissioner; Ambassador Jorge T. Lapsenson, Consul General of the Argentine Republic; Frank Ustar, Trade Commissioner–Swiss Business Hub USA; Frank Kaiser, Head of Country Desk: India, Japan and Korea; Düsseldorf Chamber of Industry and Commerce; Wang Yongpu, Ambassador to Australia from The People's Republic of China, and former Consul, Economic and Commercial Office–San Francisco for his insight, knowledge, conversations, and friendship.

I would like to acknowledge the numerous industry advisors, attorneys, accountants and bankers, especially Rob Dellenbach, David Stevens, Eric Lee, Fred Greguras, and Tom Spott, who assisted in providing content for the book through our conversations regarding their areas of expertise.

Finally, to my mentors, advisors, family and friends: Rod Davis and Gil Neff, who were ahead of their time in looking to the future of business. They prepared the groundwork for me to look at everyday situations in a totally different and unique way. To the late Thomas Pasenow for his friendship and guidance; and to my wife and muse, Caren, my first editor, confidant, and critic; to her this book is dedicated.

Contents

Foreword by Bob Karr

Competing for Global Dominance outlines the issues that entrepreneurs and businesses face as they compete in a world marketplace no longer hindered by time or distance. Today's entrepreneurs have the advantages of worldwide social media, faster transportation, cheaper labor, and financiers anxious to invest in good ideas. This has all led to a new age of globalization.

After World War II, an American migration began when businesses set up shop in Europe and Asia looking to expand their influence overseas. Silicon Valley sprang to life in the 1960s, converting orchards into office buildings, and the start-up, high-tech community was born. The international expansion that followed brought together people of diverse backgrounds—Asians, Europeans, South Americans, Israelis, Indians, and others—into groups pioneering new product development and marketing strategies in order to bring new innovative products and services to market.

The Silicon Valley success model transformed groups of individuals and businesses from around the world. Using social networking, it is accelerating the communications process through the use of Facebook, YouTube, LinkedIn, and LinkSV. This collaboration expanded influence and market share by developing new ways of doing business.

Competing for Global Dominance addresses the possibilities with practical information and first-hand knowledge. It demonstrates thought leadership from the perspective of a practitioner who works with entrepreneurs and companies from around the world to position them for endurance and expansion in the new world of globalization. *Competing for Global Dominance* is a unique work that brings together the pieces of the puzzle for entrepreneurs and companies alike to compete on the international stage.

Bob Karr, Founder and CEO
Link Silicon Valley, LLC
Linksv.com

I was on my first business trip to Japan to present a keynote address at an international conference on Customer Relationship Management to over six hundred Japanese business executives. Presenting to CEOs and other corporate executives had become "old hat" because I was doing several customer briefings weekly back in the States as well as other presentations around the world. My responsibility at the time was to evaluate our partners' technology to determine if it was a good fit for the company. If the opportunity presented looked good, I would begin negotiations to bring the technology in house for future use by our customers. Accomplishing this objective required me to meet with business executives worldwide to present new technology we offered and explain how best to use it in solving their company's business problems.

During this trip I had the opportunity to visit the Akihabara district in central Tokyo. The Akihabara is famous for its hundreds of electronics stores of various sizes, from small "mom and pop" stores to large stores like Sofmap, offering the newest in computers, cameras, televisions, mobile phones, and other home appliances. It was like Christmas in July, except that most of the electronics on sale were only suited for use in Japan and were not yet available in the United States. It would be another two to three years before some of these products would be available in the States. Most would never make it to America at all.

This was the situation I repeatedly found myself in during my international travels. I felt like Marco Polo returning to Venice from his travels to the Far East trying to explain the wonders that he encountered but unable to bring these treasures home with him. For me it would be new and different products from South Korea, China, Belgium, Denmark, Israel, and other countries where they were already in use but unavailable in the United States. I knew that if these products were available in the U.S. they could present destructive competition for local manufacturers who were becoming complacent in releasing new and innovative products for the American consumer. The U.S. market would provide these foreign suppliers the opportunity to have a greater influence on the global stage, if they would only take the risk.

Even more enlightening was how the use of new technology in the world's emerging markets was outpacing the United States. During a business trip to Culiacan, Mexico, in the late 1980s, I participated in what was to become a vital leap of innovative change in telecommunications in this Third World nation. In this coastal area east of the Sea of Cortez, best known for its rich rural farmland and plentiful crops, the government was implementing a wireless communication service available for business and individual use. Working for a jointly owned U.S. and Mexican company trying to get new high speed communications to our data center was nearly impossible, due to the amount of time required and prohibitive construction costs quoted by the local telephone company. Their solution was to leapfrog the current structure and use wireless technology, reducing the need to expend vast sums of money upgrading their existing infrastructure. My observations in Mexico as well as other countries was that their governments and their leading companies were moving quickly with the implementation of new and cost-effective technologies, while back in the United States our congressional representatives in Washington as well as the Federal Communications Commission were still arguing about fixed pricing and monopoly control of the telecommunications infrastructure. The United States was late to the party!

I realized that the groundwork laid by the U.S. Founding Fathers was being destroyed by our current federal regulators, who haven't grasped the scope of market dynamics. When faced with dramatic change, our forefathers knew intuitively what a generation has to learn to stay competitive and to survive. Our current state of world affairs provides us the opportunity to reach back into history to identify the business trends that have propelled economic development and to use this knowledge for our own preservation. I am reminded of the insight of Winston Churchill when he said, "The further backward you look, the further forward you can see."

I have met many executives who recognize their lack of market knowledge to compete successfully in international trade. I am mystified that they are not concerned about whether they have the right products, supply chain, or a personal network of contacts, which are all critical components of long-term business performance. In my experience, those executives who understand the changes that are occurring worldwide and take advantage of these new business conditions will better increase their chances for winning. Those who don't (or who go against the trends in the market) will usually struggle for market share, and then ultimately fail.

This reality was best exemplified by a Swedish executive to whom I was introduced who wanted to expand his company to the United States by relocating one of his top employees to Silicon Valley. He was coming here without knowing anyone in the United States, let alone in the San Francisco Bay Area. This individual was expected to go out and make cold calls to prospective customers throughout the U.S. to bring in orders for the company's Internet development work. As months went by without any orders, it became apparent to the CEO that his method of prospecting for new business was not working. He once said to me, "I don't know why our calls are not returned and why we cannot get in to see these executives. After all, we have an excellent reputation throughout Europe." After six months without any results to show for their efforts, he packed up and returned home empty handed.

Time after time I have seen foreign executives land on the shores of America believing that they can conquer the new world like Columbus and return home successful and wealthy. Even though Europe and other countries are skilled in creating technologies, they are not very effective at generating revenue from them. Like the Swedish executive, foreigners do not realize that the U.S. market is not like the images gleaned from watching American movies and television. Most executives fail to appreciate that business is built on personal connections and that cultural trust needs to be cultivated prior to setting foot on the airplane. The Swedish executive should have started developing his connections while still in Sweden, using online social and business networks to establish a solid contact base. He did not. He was ill-informed of how best to accomplish this undertaking in a profitable manner. To their detriment, most executives have not invested enough time and effort developing a market strategy, let alone the tactics required for growing their business in this connected world.

In fairness, American executives working overseas face the same challenges and may possess similar preconceptions that foreign companies follow the same customs and culture as American organizations.

Foreign associations who cater to emigrants from their own countries such as Korea Trade Promotion Corporation (KOTRA), Japan External Trade Organization (JETRO), British American Business Council, and German American Business Association, etc., can assist them in getting a foothold in the target country. All of these organizations have varying degrees of success.

To compete and thrive in the 24/7 global market becomes the foremost goal for businesses as well as their governments. As emerging global companies become a greater threat to non-global companies, a shift is occurring in operations where work flows to those countries, where it will be efficiently produced at the lowest cost with the objective of high quality. Through the interaction of people, companies, and governments, globalization brings change to societies from increased trade, investment, and the spreading of ideas through popular culture. The issues facing these businesses are not technology, as the Swedish executive discovered. He should have left his perceptions of America behind and found a way to enter a country that has customs, traditions, buying habits, and goals that are different from his own.

For this book I have brought together my experience working with hundreds of companies in the U.S. and around the world. *Competing for Global Dominance* brings to light the firsthand problems of what worked and what did not for these companies to establish a foundation for their products and technologies in this open and dynamic market. Whether it is in the United States or in another country, the basic concepts of market entry remain the same. How it is executed makes all the difference.

Each country over time has developed their own set of trade laws, methods of taxation, tariffs, and customs for doing business. I have used the United States of America, particularly the entrepreneurial culture of Silicon Valley, as the basis for this work because this market has best exemplified the culture that propelled innovative growth for the last half century.

1 The World Has Always Been Flat

Those who face the unprepared with preparation are victorious.
Sun Tzu

Global trade is not new; neither is globalization. Trade between countries has been going on for thousands of years. Consider the early camel caravans trudging across the deserts of the Middle East carrying their goods to far off exotic places. Then there were the golden ages of Greece and Rome, followed by the colonial eras of the British, German, Belgium, Portuguese, Dutch, French, and Spanish with colonies around the world established for the purpose of trade and wealth creation. Today, thanks to modern technology, for the first time in human history the world marketplace is open 24/7. The "sun never sets" on the world market.

For the entrepreneur, the entire world is now within reach in ways that weren't possible a few years ago. Venturing into the arena of global trade presents both opportunities and challenges for businesses, whether it is olive oil from Crete, food supplements from Germany, perfumes from France, software from Denmark, electronics from South Korea, or consumer goods from China.

The entrepreneur's challenge is influential; dominant cultures such as the United States have a significant impact on the behavior of people in other areas of the world. People are not uniform in their behavior; to understand how to compete, we need to leave our perceptions behind and find new models for entering these markets that have different buying habits from our own. This can be done through the use of online stores, interactive Web sites, video, and public relations techniques. The question is: How will the entrepreneur take advantage of today's cultural market transformation and generate revenue from it?

Identifying global trends and developing strategies to manage and execute them are vital to corporate success. Throughout history, centers of business activity, whether in fifteenth-century Venice, seventeenth-century Amsterdam, or contemporary Hong Kong, have shifted profoundly, not just globally but also regionally. As a consequence of technological advances over the last four decades, demographic shifts in the population have resulted in a massive realignment of global economic activity. These demographic shifts have affected workers in developed countries with layoffs, towns losing population (and gaining new immigrant populations), and companies manufacturing product that is no longer relevant to the needs of the market. This is not a new phenomenon. In the seventeenth and eighteenth centuries, the Dutch were perhaps the most economically wealthy and scientifically advanced of all European nations, but eventually they could not compete with the British or Spanish. Recently this same pattern is playing out with the massive modernization of China's eastern seaboard, where the population is leaving the interior and migrating east for employment.

With globalization, industries will shift even more dramatically than in the past. Shifts within regions are as significant as those occurring between nations. Average citizens are struggling to understand what is happening to their way of life and to the jobs they assumed would provide retirement security. They now find themselves forced to compete unprepared in a global marketplace.

The customer landscape has also dramatically changed with the advent of globalization. Social and business networking Web sites have expanded significantly as new ways are found to exploit the capabilities of these networks. This is great news for those who want to start and grow a business because almost a billion new consumers will enter the global marketplace in the next decade. For those emerging markets that have the right attributes, economic growth will push them beyond their current standard of living to where they will begin to spend on discretionary goods. It has been estimated that over the next decade consumer spending power in emerging markets will increase from $4 trillion to more than $9 trillion,[1] almost the current spending power of Western Europe. Shifts within consumer segments in developed economies will also be intense, as it is estimated that the Hispanic population in the United States alone will have the spending power of $1 trillion. We are also seeing an increase in consumer spending in China for goods and services; brand-name international products are especially in demand. More importantly, consumers have access to product and pricing information from manufacturers, no matter where they reside.

A unique behavioral transformation is occurring, which encourages us to communicate and work together with others around the world. Not only can we develop casual relationships with others, we can collaborate on the development of new products and services. We can also market, promote, buy, and sell goods online and have them shipped to us from anywhere. We are forming interconnected virtual communities of business and social relationships through online sites such as LinkedIn, MySpace, Facebook, Alibaba, HiTechCare, and others. More than two billion people worldwide now use mobile phones, and the numbers are increasing daily. You can audioconference or videoconference anywhere in the world for free on the Internet. There are one billion or more searches on Google, Yahoo, Ask, and Microsoft's Bing per day, and over half of these inquires are not in English. In a few short years, China has become the fastest growing country of Internet users in the world.

For companies to become successful in their target markets they will need to identify and appreciate the differences of their diverse consumers. History has shown that only a select few companies know how to initially deal effectively with this type of transformation. I am reminded of a German businessman residing in the United States who was unable to apply his knowledge of cultural differences in negotiations with a Chinese company. During the negotiation session, he tried to make them aware that what he was requesting in a way of

---

1. U.S. Bureau of Labor Statistics

a commission would not hurt their business or their revenues. When the German businessman was unable to convince his Chinese counterparts of the value he was bringing to them, he abruptly got up from the table and said, "We cannot come to a satisfactory conclusion," and stomped out of the meeting, to the surprise and embarrassment of all parties. The Chinese are accustomed to open and cordial dialogue first as they develop the relationship. Needless to say the relationship was not established and trust not gained. The German businessman lost the deal but even worse was the negative impression that spread throughout the Chinese company's business network informing them not to deal with this individual or his company in the future.

As with individuals, governments need to deal effectively with future transformation. This was dramatically illustrated when the city of Oakland, California, lured shipping away from neighboring San Francisco due to the unwillingness of the longshoremen's union to agree to the installation of modern container cranes for unloading cargo ships. This devastating loss of its container shipping business is one reason that San Francisco is now primarily a tourist town.

Entering any foreign market to establish a business for sales or seeking venture funding isn't easy. Most non-U.S. trade and economic commissioners will confirm that only five percent of their early stage companies that try to enter the United States market are successful. The remaining ninety-five percent have difficulty establishing themselves after one year. Those companies trying to acquire financing to grow will find it more difficult without a financial backer that will bankroll the company in its early development stages. This occurs even with chambers of commerce, trade and economic missions, innovation centers, foreign incubators, and a host of other organizations established after World War II to foster trade and economic development.

The Challenges of Global Trade

There are challenges facing any business entering a new market. These challenges include:

- **Increased start-up costs.** Entering any market requires short-term expenses for items such as travel, production, office space, sales and marketing materials, staff acquisition, product packaging, legal, accounting, business setup costs, relocation, and customs duties.

- **Level of commitment and time.** It will take effort and resources to establish and maintain a presence in a foreign market both to become established and to effectively grow the business. It may take years before a significant return on investment can occur. Most early stage companies do not have the sufficient resources to survive past two years.

- **Cultural differences.** Differences in language, culture and business practices in the target market(s) need to be understood and respected.

- **Unfamiliar regulations.** Foreign governments require a myriad of documentation from exporters that can present enormous challenges. Legal, accounting, and tax issues need to be addressed.

- **Accessibility.** Global trade requires ease of access to customers who are in different time zones, which will require new and flexible business and operating models to handle these changes.

- **Trust.** People like to do business with those they know and can trust. Trust takes time to foster. Even though a physical presence and face-to-face meetings are required, making your business known through social and business networking sites can assist in this process.

- **Risk of asset loss.** Security of information, intellectual property, and physical assets are a growing problem as companies expand overseas.

- **Competition.** There will always be competition for a part of the profits. Familiarity with the competition in the target market and their strategy for expansion is critical to know before entering an unfamiliar market. The only sustainable competitive advantage comes from developing and marketing new and innovative products before the competition does.

I have found that there are numerous ways to reduce the risks and increase the probability of market entry success. Leveraging expert knowledge of global trends, use of efficient business processes and practices, and understanding the unique consumer characteristics of the market are the basis for sustainable advantage in any established or emerging market.

Market Characteristics

Global trade requires a process of internationalization and localization where products such as Coca-Cola, McDonalds, BMW, and Nabisco appear familiar in each target country. Messages that sell product, create awareness, or convey a need are now able to reach with ease any consumer anywhere in the world. The challenge for today's budding companies is to bring these messages and cultural differences together successfully to create value for these new global customers.

A great deal of uncertainty exists in the global economy. Competitors are emerging in every industry and in most cases across local and international borders that were once thought to be impenetrable. Company insight of their customers is the only continually reliable competitive advantage for any organization. Relevant intelligence through market research is needed from distributors and other service providers to better understand how a product will be accepted. A clear understanding of the unique interactions of each market segment is imperative for business survival.

The process of adapting a product and message for these markets requires more than just localization to meet cultural acceptance; it needs to be universally recognized. Once, after clearing customs at Milan's Malpensa Airport, I spotted a large billboard in Italian advertising Sun Microsystems' high-end servers. I later saw this same advertisement at a subway station in Tokyo, only this time it was in Japanese with a backdrop of Mount Fujiyama. Same product, localized for each targeted country.

A global outlook is required to establish brand awareness and communicate the essence of the product across all countries. Innovative ideas travel well and are necessary to keep pace with foreign firms that are quick to copy and ready to enter your market and possibly weaken your sales. Such was the case during the Middle Ages when minor rulers often banned each others' merchants from entering their ports. This practice encouraged privateers on both sides to raid the shipping of their adversaries at will.

Throughout history merchants spoke languages such as Arabic, Latin, and Spanish. Modern executives are shaking hands, bowing, or presenting business cards in a formal manner while conversing in English that is accented with Mandarin, French, Japanese or Spanish. In truth, they are all twenty-first century industrialists.

Entrepreneurs and executives of newly emerging companies need to talk to the movers and shakers who are determining where the world is going and influencing the outcome. Those individuals can't do that if everyone in the room isn't speaking the same language. Networking is a way to begin, but it is only the beginning. Going out and exploring those markets and talking to the key influencers firsthand is imperative!

While insight derived from cumulative experience remains highly prized, the demands for growth require that insights be drawn from a deeper and broader experience. These insights must then translate directly into meaningful action. Going global in this economy requires greater sensitivity for the intended consumer by those who clearly understand the customers' buying behavior.

There is ample evidence of the rewards awaiting those who can break across boundaries and unite ideas. Success comes to those who can make the leap. These same companies are now searching the world for countries that can provide them the lowest cost structure for their operations. They now go to China for manufacturing, India for programming, and Thailand and Malaysia for inexpensive labor and resources.

Attributes of the International Business Environment

Companies are looking for dynamic economic regions with specific demographic characteristics like those of California's Silicon Valley, Boston's Route 128, Hertzelia Pituach in Israel, Hong Kong, and the Pearl River Delta area of China in order to maintain their global competiveness while growing their market share. These companies are looking for countries, cities, and partner companies who share their global ambitions. Each has attributes to create an international business environment with investment opportunities and low-entry barriers providing elements for sustainable growth. There are many areas in every country that profess to have robust economic development plans to help foreign companies to setup business. Most may have the economic incentives available but are not attuned to what their prospects are looking for and how best to provide it. There are very few companies with global ambitions that will succeed outside of these areas because the technology talent is not located there. But the needs go beyond talent. Companies are looking for:

- A workforce that is educated, flexible, adaptable and willing and able to learn new processes and produce at a reduced cost;

- Potential employees who are educated in math, science, and engineering who can add immediate value;

- A cooperative government that will work together with business, share their ambitions, and reduce bureaucratic barriers; that wants to be globally competitive; and that can make market entry easier and quicker for foreign businesses;

- An educational system with modern curriculum, international focus, multi-lingual at all levels, and with universities located nearby;

- Tax stability for planning, investment, and operational purposes with accounting standards and no capital restrictions;

- Transparency and stability in the rule of law with the capability to protect intellectual property and patent rights;

- Modernized, expanding environmentally focused infrastructure with electrical power, clean water, roads and ports to support new business while fostering sustainable growth;

- Developed and expanding ecosystems of suppliers, educators, bankers and customers close to air and sea ports for cost reduction and speed-to-market;

- A vibrant multinational local community attracting and bringing people together in a social setting from anywhere in the world;

- Reliable and secure banking systems with international standards of reporting and accountability; and

- No taxes or limited import, corporate and sales tax structures to foster trade and corporate growth.

Low-cost manufacturing countries are now experiencing the same problems with their local and multinational companies as the West has experienced. As their country's cost of living increases, so does the cost of labor, goods, services and production. At some point a company will look to move its manufacturing to lower cost areas. China is now concerned that the cost of manufacturing operations on their eastern seaboard is increasing too fast. They have a goal to develop their country's heartland to reduce the cost of production, all the while offshoring to Malaysia and other countries.

The goal for the emerging company is to reduce the likelihood that anyone else will gain a competitive advantage. The differences in market knowledge and the speed to open up new markets will make the difference for achieving global dominance.

Fifth century historian Herodotus noted in his own time that "human prosperity never abides long in the same place." Many of the cities that were majestic in his day became comparatively unimportant. Today, one only has to look at the former industrial cities in the United States such as Detroit, Michigan, and Akron and Youngstown, Ohio, to name a few that are now identified as the "rust belt" cities to see this phenomenon playing out in our lifetime. These cities lost most of their reason for existence when their leading industries relocated to cheaper areas of production, usually overseas. What remains are individuals clinging to what's left of the local economy, unwilling to adapt to the new realities of the situation they now find themselves in.

A major transformational shift is occurring worldwide and creating sustainable changes in behavior of individuals and organizations through the use of the Internet. The global reach of the Internet has been the catalyst for social and business networking having a greater influence on how business is conducted. Social networking depends on a high pass-along rate from person to person, which accelerates outward to a large number of contacts. We now have 24-hour world news coverage, low-cost air travel, and enhanced global transportation systems such as UPS and FedEx that contribute to this transformation. The result is that global trade is becoming more dynamic as old companies begin to weaken and fade away and new companies emerge to take their place.

Identifying why a nation, a city, state, or a company prospers over time and how to maintain this prosperity remains highly relevant today. Which countries and companies will end up being the world's leaders in technology, innovation, and manufacturing has yet to be determined.

2 The Elements of Global Trade

Merchants have no country. The mere spot they stand on does not constitute so strong an attachment as that from which they draw their gains.
Thomas Jefferson

There are many reasons why companies wish to expand globally. Some are faced with small domestic or limited markets for their goods and services. Others are faced with rapidly changing technology and must consider internationalizing their business in order to sustain higher growth rates and a greater return on investment. Those who wish to reduce operating expenses seek markets where production can be done at reduced labor and material rates. To flourish in the future, emerging growth businesses will have to consider whether to do business outside of their home country.

Executives wishing to expand globally will have to focus on tailoring their products and services to fit local tastes while developing a recognizable brand in these countries. Think of Coca-Cola, which is available in almost every country in the world. You can find it in major cities as well as remote jungle villages. Coke is an internationally recognizable brand that changes the formula to the taste of the population it is serving. Having a product in a remote village doesn't always increase profits or market share; it may only be for image and reputation purposes. Developing a global brand is risky, and getting it to market can be perilous.

While working for a leading U.S. food retailer with operations in the Kingdom of Saudi Arabia, I became aware of an incident that occurred between the retailer's country manager and a member of the royal family. It all stemmed from the family member wanting to sell small, inferior quality bananas to the retailer. The country manager turned down the royal's request to purchase his produce, explaining to him that the stores were selling higher quality brand named bananas which customers demanded. Within two days of the rejection of the bananas, the country manager got a call late in the evening informing him that if he didn't wish to be jailed for insulting a member of the royal family, he had better leave the country immediately. The manager left the next morning on the first flight out of the country.

As demonstrated, there are risks in entering any emerging market, especially the "BRIC" countries of Brazil, Russia, India, and China. It is unknown whether these markets will continue to flourish for foreign products or if they will rely on their own manufacturers to supply their growing needs. With China and India accounting for nearly 40% of the world's population,[2] foreign manufacturers want to exploit this demographic. To their detriment they have discovered that their products don't fit with the local styles and tastes. For software manufacturers to be successful in emerging markets, their programs have had to be localized for language and cultural differences in the country where they intend to market and sell their products.

Because of the size and diverse populations of India and China, their markets, like the American market, have grown too large for a direct entry approach. Companies such as Wal-Mart have acquired local retailers as an indirect approach to establishing a beachhead in their targeted countries. An indirect approach may offer the best potential for early success and can be used as a springboard for deeper market

---

2. Population Division of the Department of Economic and Social Affairs of the United Nations

penetration. Companies that do not take advantage of the opportunities available in emerging market countries will face an irreparable threat to their existence in the coming years.

Social marketing sites that provide massive information sharing on the Internet for free are creating demand and business leads in their communities around the world. With the advent of these global communities, individuals of similar interests are now connected through technological applications such as Facebook, MySpace, YouTube, LinkedIn and a plethora of others. Those who socialize and do business using these networks have similar tastes in products, outlooks and values. Barack Obama, in his campaign for President of the United States, used Facebook with six million fans and Twitter with 780,000 followers to effectively market himself into the highest office in the land. Is it any wonder that leading international corporations such as Coke, Bayer, and IBM use this media as part of their marketing and sales strategy? With 112 million blogs, 200 million Facebook accounts, and 36 million users on LinkedIn, social media sites are a powerful growing way to connect with customers and partners around the world.

Each company has constructed a media platform to reach an audience for their products and services. With social marketing, the nature of product acceptance has changed dramatically, bringing entertainment and information together to source goods and services. In the United Sates it has been estimated that Internet advertising in the next five years will increase by 83%, while television and newspaper advertising will decrease by 11% and 42%, respectively.[3] Global business will have to enter these subgroups of customers regardless of their different nationalities and languages to sell and promote their products.

The more people who belong to these communities, the more useful the group becomes. Social media platforms enable companies to reach customers with focused information quicker than with conventional media. The capability to have real-time interactive conversations provides instant feedback on issues that affect a company. People want to interact with like-minded individuals whether for business or in social networks. What results is a uniformity of behavior across the community bringing these groups of individuals and their countries closer together through trust and understanding.

---

3. CMO Council

Business owners who believe that they are getting a substantial return on investment (ROI) from the use of social media Web sites will spend the necessary time to manage them. By doing so, they are building bridges to the world with people from different cultures while influencing changes in consumer buying habits. They also have a focused community available for strategic marketing and sales that can be used to analyze how their product will best fit the group's demographics. The goal of participating in a network community is to leverage the group's knowledge and resources for sustainable advantage. Working within these communities can create dramatic productivity gains for any company contemplating international business.

The integration of social media with traditional methods of marketing and selling will become relevant as more companies expand into foreign markets. Local methods of doing business will change as social media expands the range of products being offered for sale worldwide. Instead of traveling to Italy to buy custom-made shoes and leather goods or to Hong Kong for custom-tailored suits, products offered online from around the world can be shipped within days to your home. It will take time for companies to discover that they have to enter these online markets just to stay competitive. In doing so, they will adapt to the new methods of marketing and selling. The information provided has to be relevant, accurate and informative to be valuable. In the not too distant future, the need to be where your customers are physically will not be required with the use of modern technology.

Talent, on the other hand, will continue to migrate to regions conducive to innovation and growth. Cities such as London, San Francisco, and Hong Kong will attract talent and create opportunities for entrepreneurs from around the world. Competition will become fierce as new competitors come into these worldwide markets looking for opportunity. To fully take advantage of social media, goods, services, and information need to be traded freely.

For the first quarter of the twenty-first century, global growth will still be powered by the U.S. consumer, even though they will spend less than they did prior to the global recession. Concurrently, China will be spearheading new consumer growth within its own country as it continues to grow its GDP and turns its policies towards domestic demand and away from exports. China may well overtake the U.S. in consumer growth before mid-century. The reason for this dramatic change is that the Chinese are becoming more affluent from their export trade and are beginning to replace diminishing Japanese and aging European markets as a global leader. China has staked its future on export-led job creation based on low currency rates, putting pressure on countries such as Mexico, India, Malaysia, and others. This deals the United States and European countries a major economic disadvantage. China's ascension as an economic power resembles the development of the United States during the 1800s, when the migration of people from the eastern seaboard westward pioneered the economic development of a growing nation. This is also the case in China today, where the migration is towards the heartland and away from Hong Kong and Shanghai on the eastern seaboard.

Well-known global companies producing items from circuit boards to refrigerators have outsourced their product manufacturing to Chinese companies to save money and increase their profits. These Chinese manufacturers that produce many different brand-name products use the same facilities as they do for their own products. Eventually they will duplicate the foreign product under their own brand to sell domestically, thereby cutting out the opportunity for their client companies to enter the Chinese market. The main difference in these products is quality and price. The foreign manufacturer is left to seek another market. It is important that companies take a critical view of this and other actions by these manufactures when entering any new market. A great product will not get you the profits you seek without a well thought out competitive marketing and partnering strategy.

Selecting the Right Markets

Unlike the guilds of the Middle Ages whose markets were limited by the ruler of the land, today's companies have greater choice in selecting their markets, whether these are local, national, or international. For the entrepreneur, this choice is just as critical for success as the guild was in its day. Commerce has expanded through Internet marketing, mass merchandising, and discount retailing instead of hanging out one's shingle or posting a bill to a tree. Entrepreneurs are developing new business models and logistic plans for handling the competition and allocating resources for market expansion.

Selecting one or two likely target markets for your product and thoroughly researching the competitive forces will drastically affect your success in entering these markets. This approach applies equally well whether you are a local retailer wishing to expand out to a new neighborhood or a high technology company wanting to expand internationally.

Companies that are looking to grow tend to select technology-savvy, fast-paced markets for product adoption. These include the United States as well as regions that are early adopters of new technology, such as Western Europe and Northeast Asia. These markets are the most lucrative and fiercely competitive, increasing the cost of market entry. Capturing these markets is often crucial as the winner in these regions usually becomes the dominant leader in that technology world-wide.

Maturing companies facilitate the community growing up around it to support and use their technology and services. The lawyers, accountants, marketers, real estate agents, and others who provide needed services to these entrepreneurs and innovative companies mark the landscape of Silicon Valley. The services provided in turn become businesses unto themselves, having mastered the ability for selling services both at home and abroad.

If you have a more mature technology or one that facilitates infrastructure growth, rapidly developing countries may be a more suitable initial market as competitive forces may not be as strong. These countries may include some of the more stable regions in South and Central America (including Brazil, Chile, and Peru), Mexico, Southeast Asia, and Eastern Europe.

Companies with products aimed at particular niche industries, such as automotive or financial services, should look at the geographic trends of that particular industry and establish themselves in the most appropriate area. Until recently, most of the U.S. automotive industry was located in the Midwest from Illinois to Pennsylvania, with its heart being in Detroit. On the other hand, the banking and insurance industries in the U.S. are located in the northeast, except for a few pockets in San Francisco, Chicago and North Carolina. Economic business regions are located around the world in such places as Rio de Janeiro,

Shanghai, Shenzhen–Hong Kong, Tokyo, London, Milan, Amsterdam, and Stuttgart, to list a few of the leading areas of economic competitiveness that power innovation.

These target markets need to be considered because they provide the resources for growth and support. In conducting market research, you need to consider which market areas have the greatest impact on the successful introduction of a product or service. Regions of a country with higher product adoption rates, along with economic health and activity, are a better choice to pursue because they show greater market stability. The market is moving away from Detroit-made automobiles, allowing foreign manufacturers to locate their facilities in the southern U.S. If these companies are your industry market segment, maybe your business should be there as a partner in the regional ecosystem.

Information is needed to determine if the target market is viable for your product. When refining the market research for new products you will need to consider these factors:

- The pace at which the population accepts new technologies

- Required service infrastructure, such as high speed and wireless communications, electric power, and transportation access

- The degree of regulation of the industry—the more regulated an industry is the harder and more time consuming it is to break into a market

- The income level of your preferred customer

- The population size and location of the customer base

- The customer's patterns of buying

- The level of competitive activity

Both state and local regulation and possible legislation relevant to your technology will affect how you adjust your marketing strategy and sales process. This is particularly relevant for biotech, pharmaceutical, and medical device companies; however, Internet and other IT product companies are increasingly affected by local privacy, censorship, and copyright laws.

When doing business overseas, the nature of the banking system as well as foreign exchange and monetary rate variations, methods of payment, and available credit all become factors in determining your target market and the profitability from that market. In addition, business ownership structures, impact of lobby groups, differences in legal systems between countries and even between state legal systems, rules of competition, patent registration and product liability all affect how you choose your target position.

It is important to take into account cultural affinity and language interpretation in developing marketing materials and in daily negotiations with customers and vendors. Even cultures that appear similar on the surface may have differences that you don't expect. Foreigners who have lived for years in America have difficulty in adapting to the way Americans do business. From the way they sell to the way they position their products to the way they handle themselves in meetings, you can always tell a European in Silicon Valley. But it goes beyond appearances to perceptions brought over from the Old World and applied to the New. It is the understanding of the languages, colloquialisms used, and the methods of negotiations, to the way they handle time. Different cultures have a tendency to clash and you have to be tuned in to the needs of each of the parties being dealt with to achieve the desired goals intended.

Developing the Business Foundation

Once the target market is selected, developing the campaign for entry will become more focused due to accepted entry methods available to you. Even though the trend has been for consistency in product development across the largest economies, product adoption still varies from country to country. This is best explained by the impact of the United States over the last half century and the adoption of English as the primary language of business. From Swaziland to South Korea, English is used to bring consistency to international business. Social media marketing takes on a new perspective as groups of interconnected people use English to promote product sales internationally. To achieve revenue in a global marketplace requires answers to the following questions.

- What positioning will produce the maximum competitive advantage?

- How will the competition respond to your actions?

- What is in it (value) for the customer, partners and employees?

- Are the logistics and supply chain required available in the targeted market?

- Do you have the support of partners and distributors to help market the sale of the product?

Answering these questions will determine the market opportunity in the niche segment that was selected. The need is to bring together a large enough portion of buyers to produce a satisfactory return for the investment. To do this requires that a company build a strong and lasting foundation for expansion to include the basic areas for company growth.

Product Expansion

First and foremost to consider is whether the product is market ready for a new country. I have spoken with CEOs who have great plans for conquering the world's markets without even having conquered their home market. I recently met an executive who wanted to bring honey into America from his native country. "Our honey," he informed me, "is the best honey in the world. Americas will love it and we can sell thousands of bottles." I asked, "Has the product been tested in your home market and has it had good customer response?" "Excellent!" he exclaimed. "The best-selling honey in the region." When I asked about how the product is selling in the rest of the country I wanted to determine the viability for expansion. He replied "No, we are local, but if we expand into America we will be famous at home and people will rush out to buy our product."

Having customers who can be referenced can make a big difference for potential buyers who want to see how well the product is doing before they make their own purchasing decision. Customers never want to assume risk, so they look to a company they can trust whose goal is to minimize the risk as much as possible. To get these assurances requires that testimonials, promotional programs and customer support are available. References can come from interested members of the social and business community, satisfied customers, and partners. All of these can provide the momentum for creating demand for the product. I asked the executive who wanted to bring honey into the U.S. if he had checked out the supermarkets in America and other specialty stores to determine where the best fit for the product would be. He said that he did not but he knew of specific grocery stores that sold products from his home country. How credible these networks of customers are, and what they would say about the honey, is of vital importance especially in the era of social media marketing. He mentioned that there was a celebrity he knew who loved the product. I asked him if he spoke to this person to possibly represent the product. He had not even thought of going this route. You see media and sports celebrities hawking everything from perfumes to cars in markets around the world. People feel they can associate themselves with celebrities by using the products those celebrities are seen using. Consumers also feel comfortable with recommendations from people they know and trust. Social media marketing is just an extension of this principle. The lesson learned is that in a competitive market you need to do your homework first. So our executive with the honey is now testing grocery and specialty stores for his niche.

Consumers have always been price-conscious and like to haggle and demand more as they look for the best deal. To see this play out you don't have to travel to Asia, the Middle East, or Mexico; you can spend time in Chinatown in San Francisco or New York. There you are expected to negotiate for the products you desire; if you don't, you insult the merchant. The time-honored game of negotiation is an important part of the transaction, leaving both parties satisfied. As the executive trying to sell honey discovered, when you have to go up against established brands, your product must have a comparable or lower price than its competitors while providing an equal or greater benefit than existing products. If it doesn't, you're not in the game.

Management and Resources

Our honey company executive could have saved himself a lot of time if he sought out advice from professionals with market- and industry-specific experience. If a company doesn't have the necessary international expertise to operate in a new market then hiring local personnel will save time and money in the long run. It is important that local executives lead the marketing effort and the allocation of staff and budget for marketing, sales and operational efforts. The budget needs to be based on realistic requirements with an estimated two-year period to get firmly established.

Market Entry Research

The example of the honey executive in not unique, but in most cases it is the norm. What he did not do was spend the time preparing a comprehensive market entry plan to determine the feasibility of his product's success. Unlike traditional market research, a market entry plan includes available sales channels, commercial and legal restraints, licensing of the product, estimated revenue streams, and costs of entry options. By researching the market opportunity in terms of future trends and growth, you can determine who you are targeting. Focusing on the niche, you can create your own opportunity to succeed.

Segmenting the market into specific submarkets will make the research process easier. You will also be able to focus on the best return on investment. Once this is accomplished, you will know where to concentrate your efforts. Recently I spoke with a CEO of an alternative energy company who was trying to determine the best direction for his company to take in the market. He was concentrating on the solar market but was unsure if he should distribute solar cells, move into the process of making thin film photo voltaic sheets, or develop solar water heaters for sale to hospitals and hotels. He presented different examples of the efforts he had in place, depending on the alternative energy requirements of the United States. He was trying to determine which solution would be the most acceptable to the public while providing the best return for his time and money. He needed to consider mitigating factors such as environmental policies, government subsidies, licensing, and any perceived dangers, which all can play a role for public acceptance. He earlier became aware that the scale and complexity of a large market like the United States may have more opportunities and greater submarket choices than those of his native country. How his customers were organized into these submarkets, by location, industry position, and immediate need, determines which ones will be the early adopters of his product. He then went on to target a shortlist of strategic and distribution partners to determine if there was a fit. In working with him, I refined his niche segment and determined who would be his target customers. We then went on to determine the effort and resources required for his company.

Competitor Analysis

Knowing your competitive position in any new market and what it takes to compete successfully is critical. Knowing realistically why you are better than your competitors and what your competitive strategy is over them will be the leveraging point for further expansion. Assessing the competition in terms of product, technology, alliances, intellectual property (IP), and barriers to entry, along with understanding how your competitors are going-to-market, are important parts of the competitor analysis.

Marketing

When doing business in Silicon Valley, it is standard procedure to ask prospective clients for a set of their marketing collateral, including their business plan, and a company presentation including financials and product information. It is best to provide this information electronically for downloading or printing to be more in depth than the materials available on a company Web site. Even in English-speaking markets there is a need to localize your marketing content to the standard accepted expressions, styles, colors and messages you want to convey to specific customer groups. Your customers, alliance partners, and other communities of interest may be the channels you will use to enter the market. Knowing the focus of the target group in terms of what they are seeking, the choices available, their "hot issues," as well as a comparison to the competition, will provide the basis for the development of the marketing materials required. Remember the honey importer? He had none of this information. Even if you wanted to buy his product, he wasn't making it easy to make a purchasing decision because he had nothing to present, not even a sample jar of honey to taste. I wasn't aware if his company had the necessary finances or budget to make entry successful.

There are different estimates for those companies who plan to enter the U.S. market. Operating expenses range from a low of U.S. $150,000 to over U.S. $1,000,000 per year just to establish a presence. A realistic financial commitment of a minimum of U.S. $250,000 will be required to cover basic first-year operating costs, not including marketing and business development activities. It will take time to ramp up operations. In the first six months, foreign companies are unlikely to be able to devote much attention to generating sales, as the focus usually is on establishing office facilities and getting to know the lay of the land. Setting up a branch office requires arranging for remote ways to manage internal operations and communications. Both effectiveness and cost will be determined by the region or city for the potential location of an office. It usually takes two years on average in a market to develop traction for product sales. Entering markets other than the U.S. takes longer and costs just as much if not more.

Sales and Distribution

Having a good product is not enough to break into a new market. You will need to market and sell the product. Using social media is a proven method of both generating demand and offering products for sale on the Web, but it is just one tool to be used. Serious sales still require a staff, either internal or outsourced in the targeted country. In the past, many companies would relocate a staff member into the targeted country to build direct sales or to establish distribution and partnership arrangements. Most of these endeavors that fail do so because the transplanted individual is not skilled in the nuances and culture of sales in their new market. Sales methodology may be the same worldwide, but the application is different in each country. As an example, there is a western tendency to express a multitude of messages to the customer. In the Japanese culture, if you were to do this it would almost always reflect badly on the company. Presenting "one face" to a customer in Japan can build confidence in your company and personal credibility.

America is made up of individuals from every country of the world; therefore, it is best to know who you will be selling to in advance. Each has a different culture and established practices on how best to sell to them. You will need to identify these before approaching them. Just because something works back home doesn't mean it will work here or for every company. Still, the question is—do you initially need your own sales staff, or should you outsource this function to those who know the market better? Outsourcing would keep your expenses down while you get acquainted with your new market.

Localization

Not all products are the same around the world. Experienced companies know they have to modify their products to meet local regulations, consumer tastes, colors, languages, and business processes. Besides the standard changes to support the target market, such as business lexicon, including spelling, jargon, measurement systems, etc., the issue may arise of how you are going to provide technical customer support. Customers expect support in their own time zone and often 24/7.

Intellectual Property

In the U.S., the law protects the owner's right to control the use and management of their intellectual property. After filing a written disclosure of an invention, the U.S. Patent Office will grant the inventor the power to prohibit others from making, using, or offering for sale the invention for a specified period of time. In the United States this is twenty years from the effective filing date. Patents can be granted on a process, machinery, a product, or a manufactured item. Correctly filing a patent application will ensure the invention or IP remains yours and will not be placed in the public domain. Patent rights can be lost merely by the non-confidential disclosure of the invention to the public, anywhere in the world, prior to the filing of the patent application.

Computer software is protected by U.S. copyright law where only the author of the software or a licensed party is entitled to reproduce, modify or distribute the software. Software companies are not selling the product, but the license to use the product; therefore, the manufacturer retains the ownership of the software. These agreements require special considerations because the license will normally establish use restrictions.

Information Gathering on Overseas Markets

When gathering information, it is imperative to look beyond the obvious and search for cold, hard evidence regarding the risks, gaps, and answers to assumptions that you may have. Identify exactly which customer groups have the "pain" or need your product will solve. It helps to experience firsthand the target country for market entry. When traveling to the U.S. to gather information, it is best to review what is required to do business, starting with your visa. According to immigration attorney Dena Wurman, the areas of information a foreign executive needs to know when entering the United States are:

1. "Apply for the correct visa. The U.S. offers many types of visas such as the "B" tourist visa. Don't plan to work on a "B" visa. An approved H or L visa will allow a person to enter the U.S. to work. An H is a working visa for an employee of a U.S. company working in a "specialty occupation." Foreign businesses not established in the United States cannot use this visa to bring employees to the U.S. Only companies that meet the U.S. government definition of parent, branch, subsidiary and affiliate qualify to petition for an L visa. Executives and employees with specialized knowledge can work in the U.S. using the L visa. You may qualify for an E-2 visa to establish a business in the U.S. if you are from a treaty country.

2. Overstaying a visa expiration date matters! Foreign nationals may not be allowed to reenter the United States for three or ten years.

3. Permanent residency can be affected by leaving the country. Trips outside the United States lasting over six continuous months may raise a red flag with immigration upon your return.

4. Maintaining permanent residence status is different from maintaining U.S. residence for naturalization purposes; some requirements overlap, but there are important differences that must be considered."

Technology Infrastructure and Adaptation Rates

A Hong Kong-based IPTV (Internet Protocol Television) company selling their technology in China and Europe was interested in the U.S. market. They were ahead of the game in their understanding of the different markets targeted for their products. What they wanted to know about the United States was how quickly the population would accept their new technology. What were the technological standards or lack of that would affect their products' adaption? In the U.S., their market would consist of TV stations at the individual, state, and local level, so they wanted to know the sophistication of their potential end users. Most important was whether the telecommunications infrastructure needed for IPTV was in place and how regulated was the industry. They were also concerned about the household Internet usage level and how the consumer was being charged. They mentioned that in other countries they faced nearly insurmountable hurdles with infrastructure issues such as electrical power, transportation, warehousing, and facilities needed to support their operations. They were proactive in thinking through the issues they would be facing.

Compare IPTV to Telkom, a South African telecommunications company whose Internet delivery time was beaten by a pigeon. The test came about when an information technology company out to prove the deplorable state of the communications infrastructure used a carrier pigeon to fly fifty miles delivering a data card strapped to his leg. It took the bird one hour and eight minutes to deliver the data, whereas it took Telkom two hours and six minutes just to deliver four percent of the information. Bandwidth in South Africa is in short supply and is very expensive compared to other parts of the world.

Level of Economic Activity

Trade occurs among all the nations on earth, but there are pre-eminent economic regions or centers where most of the activity takes place. These are based on a country's income, investment, and level of competitive activity, as well as population size, location, and patterns of consumption. Companies located in less populated countries have to expand beyond their borders if they intend to grow their business.

Political Systems

The nature of the political system, degree of nationalism and the stability of the government all play a role in the expansion of global trade. Whether a country is open to fair and equitable trade and international commerce and its relations with other countries can determine your success in these markets.

Financial Systems

The structure of the banking system, currency conversion, rate variations, and exchange policies play a key role in getting payment and establishing credit. It is advantageous to know how your customers prefer to pay for goods and services and if online banking and billing systems are available in your target country. Checks are still a very common form of payment and not all countries have credit card acceptance among their population.

There are two major challenges in dealing with the financial systems in a new market according to Eitan Sapir, First Vice President, Bank Leumi USA:

> The first is the lack of credit history, building credit history takes time. Founders, executives, and engineers are often surprised that the lack of credit history prevents them from obtaining credit cards or receiving other types of credit facilities. The second is cross-border activity. The typical startup coming to the U.S. will have activity in both countries. These activities require cross border transactions including opening accounts to non-domestic entities, currency conversions and hedging and maintaining accounts.

Banking Institutions such as Bank Leumi and others that operate in foreign countries help their customers by using extensive networks, allowing their customers to leverage their global reach. "Opening a U.S. bank account is the first step," according to Eitan, "so we make this step very easy for them. We can have the account opened while the executives are still in their home country, so when they arrive in the U.S., the account is already open and everything is set for them."

Legal Structure

Establishing a business presence in any foreign country requires expert legal advice. Due to the litigious nature of the United States, it is particularly important that you obtain legal counsel before venturing into any corporate or commercial endeavor. It should be kept in mind that firms skilled in general corporate law are not necessarily good at handling patents, litigation, or immigration. Remember, a deal is not done until it is signed as a contract. Attorneys can help you with incorporating and determining the best structure for international and local business.

"Foreign companies consistently make legal mistakes," according to Michael Moradzadeh Esq. of Rimon Law Group:

> Often foreign companies take a wait and see attitude hoping that they can cross certain legal bridges when they need to. However, this often ends up costing the companies a lot more because it is always much cheaper to do something right from the beginning rather than having to fix it last minute. For example, it is crucial to make sure organizational documents, licensing and employment agreements are drafted to ensure long-term growth and asset-protection, while also taking into account tax efficiency and optimization for financing and exit strategies.

Culture, Customs, and Practices

Executives need to be aware that cultural similarities exist, but there are also very large differences. Language, images, and graphic symbols must be correctly handled to communicate the right message to conduct business and carry on trade. Such was the case of UNICEF using an image of disembodied shaking hands on the sides of their relief trucks and being confounded when no one would come near the trucks to receive much needed supplies. The image was meant to symbolize cooperation between people but only frightened the superstitious locals.

In another instance, there was an individual who approached U.S. distributors trying to sell "table blankets" to them. He was turned away because the distributors knew that this individual had not spent the time researching the market and probably would not be effective in selling the product. This could have been avoided had he simply used the word "tablecloth" to describe his product. What he discovered was that even cultures that appear similar on the surface may have differences that you don't expect. Culture, customs, and practices all play a role in successfully establishing a presence and conducting business.

3 The Myth of American Competitiveness

Europe was created by history.
America was created by philosophy.
Margret Thatcher

For many non-U.S. companies the first market of choice outside of their home country is the American market. As stated by President Calvin Coolidge, "the chief business of the American people is business." Since its founding the United States has been primarily focused on trade and business. Yet today, America is facing a new economic challenge never before faced in its roughly two hundred year history. In recent years foreign manufactures such as Sony and Toyota posed and remain a threat to American companies. Today an even bigger threat to American companies is China-based companies. How will American businesses compete head-on with China? It is not only American companies that need to answer this question, but any foreign company that wishes to compete for the U.S. dollar as well as using the U.S. market as a springboard to the world.

What Makes the U.S. Market So Different?

The U.S. market is the largest open market in the world with the buying power of 308 million people plus significant global influence. Many characteristics of this competitive market are based on geography, country of origin, age, education, and income distribution. Not only is the United States large in land mass, taking over ten hours to fly from Maine to Hawaii, but diverse in culture, from high-end Manhattan couture to Hilo Hattie clothing in Hawaii.

Over the centuries the United States has become an unequaled global importer of a wide variety of the world's products, primarily to satisfy the needs of its growing immigrant communities. These communities grew and created their own products and methods of selling to neighboring immigrants such as the Irish and Italians in New York City. But what became evident were different selling patterns between peoples. Going to a modern supermarket in America and strolling down the ethnic food aisle, you will find entire sections devoted to Italian, Asian, Mexican, and kosher foods.

It's easy to find Mexican, French, Chinese, Thai, or Japanese restaurants in your local American neighborhood, unlike most of the rest of the world, where it is almost impossible (although I did discover a wonderful Chinese restaurant in Rome directly across the street from the Vatican).

There are three primary methods of selling in the United States, as well as in other countries in the European Union, Asia, and South America. These are:

- direct sales—individually hired salespeople;

- indirect sales—sales through distributors and retailers; and

- Internet sales—through online Internet Web sites and social media.

Because so many companies in the world want to market their products in the United States, competition is fierce and only the fittest and most astute will survive. America is fertile with innovative ideas, prospects of obtaining wealth for creative entreprenuers, companies that act on ideas, and investors who take the risk after imaging the possibilities. Globalization has been mainly the spread of Americanization through worldwide appeal of products and services. For example, due to their popularity, Levi's jeans can be used in trade in numerous foreign countries.

Having a diversified population helps America in marketing goods worldwide as well as for foreign companies marketing to America. One third of the people, over 100 million, are identified as minorities in America, such as Hispanic, Chinese, Indian, Japanese, and others from around the world. Each of these groups brings diverse back-grounds, cultures, languages, and buying habits. These pockets of mi-norities enable marketers to test new products locally rather than entering each foreign country. The foreign-born population in America is approximately 12.5%, while 14.8% of the population is Hispanic (44 million individuals and growing), 4.4% are Asian, and 12.4% are African American.[4] The largest numbers of immigrants continue to flock to six states. These are California, New York, Texas, Florida, and New Jersey, all coastal states, and Illinois in the Midwest. One-half of the foreign-born population in the United States is from Latin America, and more than one-fourth is from Asia.

For those few companies that are successful in the U.S. market the rewards can be substantial. By winning the American market, the op-portunities for entering other international markets follow. America tends to be a trendsetter in such industries as motion pictures, search engine technology, Internet marketing, viniculture, networking, and a host of other industries. Where the evolution of business has been linear for most of the world, in America it has been much more impul-sive. That is why there are so many more opportunities here. The scale of the U.S. is so large that a degree of change can mean millions of dollars.

Some CEOs believe that because they are successful in their home country they can conquer this New World, but they are in for a rude awakening. These CEOs need to take a realistic and grounded approach to their market analysis well before they consider entering the U.S. The time and resources initially spent performing this analysis can pay off generously in the future if done by someone both familiar

---

4. U.S. Bureau of Labor Statistics

with the product and the U.S. market. The first consideration is to develop a concise market entry plan for the United States. There are plenty of companies and organizations nationwide that can assist in putting this plan together. It is important that the senior management in your company lead the overseas marketing effort and support the allocation of people and budget for these marketing efforts. I cannot stress enough how having a realistic budget for international business development can make the difference between success and failure. In doing your market research, it is well worth remembering that the customer buys the satisfaction that a product brings.

For all the attention bestowed on the United States, the vast majority of foreign businesses are clueless in understanding its market or how to leverage their position. If this is the case in the United States for these companies, then it would become even harder to establish themselves in India or China due to their restrictive nature. The U.S. market is too large and complex for an all-out direct marketing assault on it unless there is sufficient capital and resources behind the campaign to sustain it nationwide. Few American companies blanket the entire U.S. market all at once. The business model for most foreign companies needs to be focused on the available niche markets where barriers to entry are lower. Here is where knowing how the competitors go-to-market becomes important. Tracking their channels and customer base for possible opportunities to move in after them is another alternative. Americans like to have choices. It never hurts to approach a competitor's customers to gather information about what is liked or disliked in their offering. Also, check on how service is provided. Service is the key to acquiring and keeping customers. IBM now leads with service and support when it goes after new customers.

This reminds me of when I was working for a leading international retailer that went out to bid for a new in-store computer system worth millions of dollars. We narrowed the contenders down to Tandem Computers and IBM, who was our primary computer vendor at the time. Tandem won the bid. The next day IBM doubled its account staff searching for ways to find new opportunities to provide service and support to hold its account. It turned out that this was a very successful strategy in the long term. IBM knows that persistence pays off in America.

In the United States foreign companies can acquire global brand recognition faster because there still remains a mystique about foreign-made products. Whether this is real or perceived doesn't matter. Leveraging it does! Häagen-Dazs ice cream, for example, which started out in the Bronx, New York, gave the company a foreign-sounding name to convey an aura of the old-world traditions and craftsmanship to their customers. Chanel No. 5 made French fashion designer Coco Chanel world famous in the 1930s, but her biggest success in the U.S. came after First Lady Jackie Kennedy began wearing her suits and American women followed her example. Chanel came up with a style that was "expensive simplicity" for the working woman; it was so elegant that it remains popular today.

To compete with the world's best companies requires foreign manufacturers to design and produce quality products incorporating the latest in technology with the leanest supply chain and manufacturing principles. It also means promoting the uniqueness of your product. Vying for recognition against numerous competitors, you need to differentiate yourself by your country or history.

It is a matter of time before China will become a pre-eminent market for foreign goods on par with the United States. China is rapidly becoming the most important market for high-end luxury goods with a thirst for consumer electronics and other technological products. To satisfy their growing demand for new and innovative products, the Chinese are shopping the United States and other western countries to find the top selling brands to bring back to their homeland. The Chinese believe that for a company to compete on the world stage they must be in the U.S. market. A Chinese businessman once mentioned to me that the Chinese look at the U.S. market as the doorway to the worlds' markets. The Chinese desire products that are in demand in the U.S. and Europe.

Companies who decide to make this journey on their own generally fail. Foreign executives don't think in terms of guides or mentors to help them through the maze of business issues. Early on they will be tested by their prospective distributors as to how they will sell and market their products. The distributors may ask:

- Are there market development funds available? If yes, how much money is available?

- What is your marketing and advertising plan? Do you plan on advertising in the newspapers, radio, or on TV?

- In which regions will you market—Los Angeles, Dallas, Chicago, New York, or Miami? Many distributors don't blanket the entire U.S. Most focus on very narrow regional markets.

- What types of channel programs will you provide your distributors? Channel programs will have to be put in place to support your U.S. distributors.

- Are your products and marketing collateral modified to meet local regulations and accepted industry language?

- Have you a plan for international marketing and sales?

- Do you have an operational budget which allows for a minimum of at least 12 months to get you started?

- What type of technical support will be provided? Customers expect support in their own time zone and often 24/7.

Having knowledge of the local laws, culture, and business practices become important as each state is independent of each other and consumer behavior varies dramatically within different regions of the U.S.

The perception of being a viable and growing company matters most. This can be accomplished by means of having a local address and phone number, an Internet Web presence, sales representatives, reference customers either here or abroad, and marketing materials in perfect English.

Getting to the appropriate channel now becomes the challenge. There are several choices available:

- Distributors

- Licensees

- Original equipment manufacturer (OEM)—typically uses a component made by a second company in its own product or sells the product of the second company under its own brand

- Value-added reseller (VAR)—adds feature(s) to an existing product, then resells it as an integrated product

Several of these approaches can be combined because they are not mutually exclusive. Together with an understanding of your target market, distribution channels, and the competitive landscape you will be in a position to shortlist strategic partners. Strategic partners may want to expand on your unique products. A good example would be lavender, which can be a key ingredient in foods, lotions, and aromatherapy. These partners may include key customers and aligned suppliers with non-competitive goals.

Living in a global economy, we are seeing that more companies need to become exporters of products or services. Companies will not have to have copious resources or an entire department devoted to exporting to make this happen. The use of the Internet along with convenient air freight makes the process easier for more small and medium-sized businesses. In the U.S. each of these companies accounts for anywhere from $30,000 to $5 million in exported goods and services each year.[5] The U.S. may be losing its "first mover advantage" to foreign companies as U.S. manufacturing has been leveling off over the last few decades creating serious outside competition. We can no longer assume that the way we conduct business will remain the same.

Adapt or Die

During an economic crisis when credit is tight, you cannot depend on customers who are having difficulty getting credit to maintain their business operations. For the surviving companies the focus is on growing the company and increasing market share both at home and abroad, as consumers will save more and consume less. We are experiencing a challenging global business environment which will result in

---

5. U.S. Government Trade Portal

stronger and leaner companies as the weaker ones go out of business and fewer companies get funded. What emerging markets offer U.S. manufacturers is the time to educate customers about the value of their products. Because they have a pool of talented service providers and workers to choose from, they are able to cut costs and shift production to cheaper manufacturing countries.

Adapting to the behavior of the consumer will help in penetrating the American market. There are certain traits displayed by most Americans and knowing these will help in how business will be conducted. Americans first and foremost tend to network more openly both in person and online than others. They also tend to network outside of their own groups with diverse individuals of many cultures. This is one of the reasons why online social media has taken off and companies such as Facebook and YouTube are doing well. You will find that Americans ask pointed questions in their business dealings. Most business people will deliver on promises and expect you to do the same. They are responsive, ambitious and achievement orientated. Americans believe that anything new is good and worth at least trying once.

I believe that Americans know how to sell, promote, and market their products and services better than anyone. Being an optimistic people, Americans see opportunity in their lives. They also believe that time is money and should not be wasted.

American business, like business around the world, has historically been based on establishing one-to-one relationships. Likeminded individuals owing to place of birth, religion, language, culture, or socioeconomics tend to associate with those who hold similar interests. In Silicon Valley alone, there are over 280 networking organizations and thousands of networking events every year where people can meet to socialize and conduct business. Many of these organizations have their own Web sites, which encourages an effective environment for soft selling and business development. For all practical purposes, business networking is conducted after normal working hours. You have to move away from your comfort zone, which means meeting people from other countries and expanding to other groups and organizations to be successful. You only have one opportunity to make a great first impression!

Americans are always looking for the next opportunity. Technology changes on a weekly basis as well as the demand. During a recent venture capital VC "pitch session" for start-up companies, held almost weekly in Silicon Valley, I witnessed just how fast investors review companies and their technology. If they don't see the answers presented immediately and completely thought out, they will move on to the next company. America is a media-enriched culture based on 30-second television commercials that quickly show a product's benefit and use. Most companies are not prepared and cannot even explain their product's benefits within the 30 second "elevator pitch," let alone summarize a market entry strategy in a five-minute presentation.

I see the same mistakes over and over again. Company executives don't understand if their solution will be accepted by the customer or even if the problem they are trying to solve really exists. No company can earn profits without a distinctive competitive advantage, especially one that is difficult for others to imitate. Make sure you have your pitch and a positioning statement that is understandable to a layperson, and that it's well-rehearsed and believable.

Service expectations in the U.S. are significantly higher than in most countries. The differentiator will be quality customer service. You will be catering to demanding customers and partners who will expect only the best. I had an associate who was living outside of Beijing and was in need of transportation so he decided to follow the local custom of using a bicycle. After making his purchase and attempting to assemble the bicycle he discovered that a main part was missing making the bicycle unusable. He returned to the store and explained the situation expecting to exchange the bicycle for a functioning one. The store's proprietor informed my associate that he could not return the bicycle but if he needed parts he could purchase a new bicycle. Not receiving any satisfaction from the store proprietor, he was left with his useless property to repair on his own. He did so by finding the needed parts online. This is unlikely to happen in the United States because the majority of retailers will exchange the merchandise if the product is defective.

Being available for meetings, presentations, and telephone calls is mandatory! You will need to overcome the distance factor and be with your customer face-to-face when required. Too many times I have seen a foreign company that would travel to the U.S. to present their company and its products then return home with no follow-up to determine interest. If there was interest, these companies did not make themselves available for further inquiries or meetings.

Americans are consummate salespeople who will expect you to "talk the talk and walk the walk." Be aggressive and straight to the point but not demanding. Be confident but not arrogant or stubborn. Arrogance or a know-it-all attitude is offensive and irritating and will lose the sale. Be open and accommodating with your schedule. By not following these suggestions, you may kill any opportunities before they begin.

A company's brand equity is the totality of the consumer's experience and perception that make the brand recognizable worldwide. This includes the quality of products and services, financial performance, community relations, customer loyalty and satisfaction. A brand should equal trust. Mercedes-Benz, Creed, and Louis Vuitton are companies that convey a high degree of brand trust, which translates into success. To build trust you need an awareness of value and an assurance of quality. A recognized brand serves as a valuable means for consumers forced to choose among an assortment of products and services in the marketplace. You see this in grocery stores all the time: a man holding a cell phone while staring at a wall of products, not knowing which one to choose until his wife says, "Honey, the blue box with the yellow stripes." It is up to the company to make sure it's *their* blue box with yellow stripes being purchased.

Branding is the essence of successful marketing where a single minded idea conveys a clear and consistent message. The goal is to build consumer awareness while changing deep-seated customer habits.

It would be the best of all worlds for the product to be so good that it doesn't require advertising. Cultural barriers can be overcome with brand positioning, developing customer trust by offering strong value. As customers develop their perception of value through a subjective process based strictly in their own needs, preferences, culture, and buying behaviors, a company's brand promises to meet those needs and consistently deliver on them.

Every business, especially a foreign company wanting to increase its presence, needs a brand champion. This can be an individual, usually the CEO (think Steve Jobs, Richard Branson, Bill Gates, and others), or a marketing firm dedicated to ensuring that a consistent message goes out to the public. Their goal is to maintain a concise message both for the employees and the public and is included in all marketing materials. Remember, inconsistency in the message generates frustration and mistrust. Consistency of the message requires:

- Knowledge of who will be using your product

- Why your customers will be using the product

- How will they use product

- What the significant demographic patterns are of these customers

Creating Value in a Commodity World

In buying a product, people usually believe they get what they pay for; otherwise, why buy the product? The goal, whether it's BMW, Apple Computer, Coca-Cola, or Rolex is to create value that people will appreciate enough to become lifelong customers, which is your best source of advertising. Think of the neighbor who every year bought himself a new Cadillac and would not dream of buying another make of automobile. One day a Lexus appeared in his driveway—why? General Motors gradually lost their dedicated following by not catering to the values of their customers. This opened a window of opportunity for foreign car manufacturers to step in and respond to those customers' needs. Buyers generally want lower cost products, so they think they are "getting a deal," while not lowering the perceived value of their purchase. The exception would be Wal-Mart and other big box stores that specialize in inexpensive products many of which are considered disposable.

With the introduction of new technology and globalized brands, competition has forced the commoditization of many products into a downward spiral to reduce the cost of goods and services. There has been a rise in replicas of luxury goods or "knock-off" products, which look like the original but are without the quality, thereby eliminating the profit for the original manufacturer.

Value-Based Strategies

Companies provide value and overcome commodity pressures by finding narrower market niches to compete in. There are customers that will pay top dollar for quality and service. Then there is the commoditization approach, where the only way to make money is by continually lowering the cost structure so that you can compete on price. You see this practiced with electronics, where the prices are constantly lowered as new products enter the market. The quality brand approach provides a high-end product that has been scaled down to fit the lower cost and a larger market. Jaguar Motors, for example, has already made this move by releasing their X Type Model referred to as the "Baby Jag." Finally, an imitator or "knockoff" product still offers quality for the money because the buyer is aware that it is not genuine, so the price fits the product. Today's business environment encourages the commoditization approach to products and services, yet sustainable advantage has come from a value-based approach.

Establishing Value

Value applies to manufacturer as well as to suppliers and finally to customers and communities of interest. Focus on the value message to emphasize what your product can do better than the competition. The difference between you and your competition should become clear. By solving the critical problem of meeting the customers' specific needs while understanding their pain factors, you will position these products in a better consumer light. If you focus on the customers "food chain," their employees, suppliers, interest groups and educate them on how they too can make money or reduce costs with your product they will begin to influence others in ways that can benefit you. Make it easy for the buyers to understand what you do and how you do it. Inform them of the product's value; don't rely on them to figure it out. Finally, by offering small, individualized value service offerings leading to a complete solution, you can gradually build trust and acceptance.

Product Value

Market value traditionally is the price that a manufacturer may reasonably expect to obtain for their product. Product value can be real if there is a tangible benefit for the purchase or perceived if the benefit derived is intangible. The reason for a specific decision by the buyer may not always be apparent to the seller when it comes to the real value of the product. It may have nothing to do with the market price of the product but more on personal satisfaction. There are accepted marketing principles which have been acknowledged by successful companies in dealing with a product's value accepted by their customers. What these companies realize is:

1. Customer accepted product value and price are the real issues that drive sales.
2. The customer defines what the value of the product is for them.
3. Product value has a narrow focus for each customer.
4. Product value and the additional significance of their services are the only real products a company can sell.
5. The market positions the product's value to the manufacturer.

The best way to sell a product is to ensure that the customer can identify a fair return for their money. The value of a customer in a business-to-business relationship is determined by revenue, market share, and client retention. Creating customer value requires a process of due diligence in researching the buyers' "pain factors" and what the manufacturer can do to eliminate these. A company can determine a customer's needs through intelligence gathering by using industry trade publications, online searches, 10K filings, annual reports, social networking sites, and blogs. The customer needs to understand what you are offering in comparison to other companies. Why should we go with you? This is the question they will be asking especially because you are new to the market. What's the difference between using your product versus someone else's product? What is needed on your part is to know the impact of the buying decision and risk, which you are trying to mitigate. It's not only what you sell; it's how you sell the product that brings it value.

All buyers will try to minimize risk and like to do business with companies they are familiar with. To position your company with new customers it is helpful to have published articles about your firm and positive comments on blogs and tweets. Producing videos about your company and your products on YouTube legitimizes your company and makes tangible what you are saying. It also can make your company the expert in a product area. Furnishing references, testimonials, and letters of recommendation from satisfied customers who can be contacted for validation adds credibility. Influential industry experts and celebrities may enhance your product's status and value worldwide. Wouldn't it be great to have Steven Spielberg, Oprah Winfrey, and others use your products! People like to associate with winners.

Never assume that buyers know you or your company's reputation. You have to educate them. To enhance your reputation, identify your best product, the one with the highest perceived value and promote it. The goal is to make it easy for prospective buyers to understand your value proposition and determine whether or not it's fair and can handle their requirements. Make it easy for them to find you and to buy from you.

The most influential brands in reality are not a creation of your marketing department but come directly from the experiences of customers. Knowing what your brand means to the customer is everything. Their experience is based on innovation and creativeness of the products features, its quality, design, and value. The most powerful force in branding is word-of-mouth and this can be generated through online communities, which help promote the brand worldwide. Developing and protecting the brand's image is critical for global brand expansion. A successful brand determines the perceived value, which in turn influences how much is charged for the product. Just hearing the names Gucci, Cristal, Bentley, Creed, Neiman-Marcus, or Cartier brings mental associations.

Winning the Value Game

By narrowing your focus to a specific target group of customers you can better maximize your efforts and resources for the best possibility of success. The old adage of: "focus on your niche until you can dominate it" still applies with any group of customers. The best way to do this would be to create expertise and value so nobody can compete with your company or would have difficulty doing so. Think of such companies as Apple Computer, Hewlett Packard, and Cisco Systems, that have created alliances and partnerships with smaller companies helping them create value for their products. These industry leaders can assist in understanding who the target buyer is and how to sell, support and deliver the product to them. By looking for new and innovative ways to solve your customers' problems and serve their needs will create new channels and opportunities.

The secret to creating value is through passion and confidence, which you can bring to the buyer while respecting the problems they are trying to resolve. Don't offer customers a new technology unless it solves their problems better than their current solution.

Chapter 3: The Myth of American Competitiveness

4 Jumping the Shark

When you discover that you are riding a dead horse, the best strategy is to dismount.
Dakota Indian saying

When is the precise moment that a company or a well-known product starts to go irreversibly downhill and loses all credibility with its customers or investors? What are the key indicators? Why didn't the company executives recognize the problem and correct it before it occurred?

How many times have we seen this situation as companies rise to power only to lose their market dominance and have another replace them. These globally recognized companies that grew to enormous size such as U.S. Steel, Polaroid, Siebel Systems and Sun Microsystems were once leaders in their field and now have either gone bankrupt or been acquired by another company. This is the process of creative destruction whereby aging and failing businesses are eliminated and newer more productive ones emerge.

Every week we see new products being advertised and placed on store shelves only to quickly disappear if sales expectations are not met. Junkyards are littered with 8 track players, Betamax, vinyl records, Sony's Walkman, film based cameras, and VCRs. Not to mention landline phones, which cellular models have replaced.

Creative destruction applies to governments as well. The Roman Empire survived for centuries but eventually fell into ruin. The British once could claim that the "sun never sets on their empire" but found themselves after the Second World War back to an island nation, the empire lost. Daily we are experiencing the constant birth and disappearance of companies and their products in the marketplace.

Over the last four decades American business believed the principle that bigger is better. Superstores like Safeway and warehouse stores like Wal-Mart, Costco, and Home Depot have grown larger carrying thousands of stock keeping units (SKUs). At one time manufacturers filled the shelves with variations of their products in all shapes, sizes, and packaging. Just walk down any isle in a Safeway superstore and you will see shelf after shelf of breakfast cereals, salad dressings, laundry detergents, etc. to fit every customer's need and lifestyle.

Manufacturers have given us so many choices that customers may feel overwhelmed. The simple chore of selecting a cereal in the grocery store becomes a battle of wills between a mother and child. The mother wants a nutritious product for her child but he may be nearing hysteria being asked to choose only one box when the Saturday morning cartoon programs advertise so many choices. Nutrition is the furthest thing from his mind. He craves what the leprechauns or tigers are selling or anything that has a sugary crunch. Yet, for all the varieties of cereal on the shelf, most are made by a small handful of manufacturers who supply their products to every grocer in America. General Mills' Wheaties cereal has been the "Breakfast of Champions" for sports heroes from Lou Gehrig to Michael Jordan. Having too many choices doesn't only apply to cereal. It can apply to hardware, software, medical devices and so much more. There are over 140,000 applications available online for the Apple iPhone. Having a large variety tends to commoditize the individual product and increases pressure on the manufacturer to reduce prices. Pricing has always been a major factor in consumer decision making. The mother in the grocery store is probably on a budget and looking for ways to reduce costs.

There are small scale manufacturers and retailers being pushed to the wayside because they are unable to compete against the buying power of larger ones. The same applies when smaller companies are targeted for a merger or acquisition. Predatory pricing from foreign competition has resulted in the primary industries either picking up and moving to lower cost production areas or going out of business altogether. Interestingly, for some small manufacturers that went out of business, their products have been recreated and relocated to places such as the Cracker Barrel Old Country Store. The favorite childhood candy you thought you would never find again is sold at the place that you stopped to have lunch. Where have these products been? What happened to the company? Were they just a fad or is the product still sustainable?

Products become exceptional when a consumer is impressed but they don't expect to be. The product goes well beyond fulfilling their expectations. It has the wow factor! When the brand conveys a strong positive message that resonates with the consumer it usually has staying power.

You just have to skim through a *Wall Street Journal* or *Financial Times* to discover which companies are in demand. The problem is having to sort the wheat from the chaff to determine what is true and what is not about these reports. Too often you read contradictory reports about the same company. The first test to find this out would be the "gut test" to determine if the information being presented in the media is accurate. Does it seem right? Does it really make sense or is it "spin" provided by the company to present itself in a good light? If it turns out to be spin the company may have already jumped the shark and is already in decline.

Many Silicon Valley companies have made claims that have turned out to be misleading to the public. A few years back Cisco executives announced that they had a state-of-the-art Internet inventory and production system that provided accurate information at a glance. They shared this system with their suppliers even though Cisco had limited visibility of their distributors' inventory and order backlog. They promoted this system to their partners and to the press. Their executives relied heavy on this system. They misread the warning signs that their sales forecasts were too ambitious. Eventually Cisco had to admit that this system was a failure resulting in Cisco writing off $2.2 billion worth of inventory.

Numerous times I participated in strategy development for a variety of Silicon Valley companies. During one meeting the CEO was anxious to let the media know how well the company was doing by stating that their newly released product would change the nature of the industry. Coming off of a bad quarter it was important to let the investors know that sales were picking up. The CEO's plan was to get the message out through business talk shows on television and the industry press. His vice president of marketing informed the CEO that what he was planning to announce in the way of product availability was premature because the products weren't ready yet. The CEO ignored the advice and went on the public relations circuit anyway spinning the new product and saying the company was meeting the analyst expectations. Did the company jump the shark? The company is still around but the CEO is hesitant to go before the press while the analysts spend more time reviewing the numbers. There are companies that are able to survive jumping the gun, but very few can survive jumping the shark.

As we have seen, one way that business will deal with uncertainty has been to ignore it. Many companies have been blindly plodding along, investing money in marketing, staffing, sales, and operations when economic times are good, only to cut back when sales and revenues are down. This cycle creates its own self fulfilling prophecy when the market picks up and companies find themselves loosing sales because they had shifted down instead of being out in front of the competition. State and local governments are also not immune to this thinking. Cities that are spending on numerous social programs are failing to help their local businesses grow. In speaking with state and local bureaucrats I found them not only to be myopic but lacking incentive programs to keep their businesses local. Their sister cities around the world are encouraging these businesses to relocate. They are providing both monetary and non monetary incentives such as free rent, high speed Internet access, tax relief, and government support.

Reasons Companies Fail

There are many reasons why companies fail, from poor management to products that are no longer accepted by the market. There tend to be seven primary reasons why companies lose their position within the market.

- Diminished satisfaction with the company and its products

- Loss of value, when customers don't perceive the benefit from the product

- Poor market positioning; the best product will not sell when others with the same benefit are selling at half the price

- Changes in technology

- Shift in the customers' perception of a company or product

- Bad press from a major incident that turns the buying public against a company such as tainted food products, automobile recalls, or lead based paint on children's toys

- Something better comes along

Poor positioning is best demonstrated by the increase in store brands versus national brands that principal retailers are carrying to increase their sales. As more retailers provide their own brands, the amount of real estate in a store dedicated to national brands will continue to diminish. Because the retailer has a higher margin on their own brands it makes sense that they would promote their own products. Shoppers in most cases will not care if the product is a store brand if the quality is equal to the national brand.

Economic hard times present new challenges as well as opportunities for those companies considering expansion globally. The U.S. is experiencing a significant down turn of imports and exports as indicated by the reduction in container traffic worldwide. This decline affects warehousing, distribution, and commercial properties all the way down the line to employment growth.

Consumer shopping behavior is changing in response to retailers modifying their methods of operation. This behavior is best exemplified through the expanded use of the Internet and the worldwide Web. Woolworths, as an example closed all of its retail stores in the United Kingdom only to be re-launched online carrying a more focused assortment of the same consumer products. The competition is fierce from such companies as Tesco PLC, Home Retail Group PLC and others who have already migrated online and have an increased their customer base.

The shopping malls have become the gathering places for the under 30 crowd. This generation uses retail stores for window shopping and when they like what they see make the purchase online. Will this leave retailers as merely catalog stores as in the early days of Sears Roebuck and Company? If so, this will affect how advertising dollars are spent. Will it be on print ads, TV, or only online? To respond to the changes in customer buying habits Sears has launched new Web sites and phone apps to reach out to those using the Internet and expand beyond their physical stores. Sears understands that e-commerce represents about 7% of the U.S. retail market and will continue to increase in the following years. They are beginning to list items from other sellers on their Web sites for a percentage of the sale, which is another innovative way to compete using the Internet.

Changes can be seen in the retail environment as shopping malls are closing and retailers are reducing the number of stocked product varieties as well as inventory on hand. This trend is occurring around the world especially in Northern Ireland where prices are falling faster than anywhere else in the world. As consumer buying habits change, retailers and their supply chain are altering their operating processes to reflect the transformation of the market as well as the expanded use of the Internet. For all the infrastructure issues, it's still about having the best products available for the customer.

What we are experiencing today through globalization is the massive disruption of the markets, both labor and capital. The difference today is that through a system of high speed communications we are now able to communicate and collaborate faster with others around the world. Because of technology supply chain methods of getting goods to market have been created and better utilized to take advantage of global capital and labor.

Retailers want to keep their inventory low and are testing new supplier's products first on their Web sites to monitor consumer acceptance before placing these product in their stores. Their goal is to simplify their operations and reduce their inventory and costs wherever feasible.

The changes in retail and in consumer buying habits brought on first by the Internet and then by social media are forcing a transformation among suppliers. Alibaba, a Chinese e-commerce company of which Yahoo is a primary stakeholder is now launching its company into the U.S. market. They broker materials to make everything from clothing to electronic parts. Alibaba matches suppliers with wholesalers very much like a virtual trade show. With more than 45 million users, of which 1.6 million are Americans, Alibaba is working to help small to medium sized businesses enter China's market by developing virtual storefronts for their member companies. More suppliers are changing their fulfillment methods to support these business changes that are affecting their distributors and importers. Risks are now being shared and consumer products are bought from overseas manufacturers on consignment versus using letters of credit or other means of payment.

The network community is buying their goods online through companies such as Amazon, eBay and Staples. Online sites such as Home Shopping Network and 430PM in the U.S. use economies of scale marketing to provide the lowest price on many brand name products for a limited period of time to their dedicated community of interest. New technology is coming to market that will make it easier for customers to locate a specific product and choose how they wish to purchase it. This could be online, through television or in retail stores.

Shoppers worldwide like social interaction and to physically examine the items before they buy them, especially high touch products such as clothing, luxury goods, food, and beverages. But people will migrate to online shopping because of time constraints, limited store selection or they are dissatisfied with their present means of shopping. The internal dynamics of companies will demonstrate how they respond to these changing market conditions and whether they continue to ride a dead horse or dismount. The red flags a company needs to watch for are:

- Expected internal or external value fails to materialize.

- Executives are unable to think long term as business needs change.

- Changes in internal business strategies.

- Slow company response to requests.

- Customer relationships are deteriorating.

- An overly optimistic attitude or arrogance in their news releases and analyst meetings.

- Poor or no communication both internal and external.

- Ambiguous or poor leadership by executives.

- Unclear operating principles and a failure to handle problems effectively.

- Poor hiring and management practices.

- Overexposure in advertising and public relations.

The single biggest reason that businesses fail is that they are unable to find a niche that is sustainable or they lost that niche to their competitors. Most companies are no different than their competition. They look the same, feel the same and from the view of the average customer, they are the same. They do not know how to differentiate themselves in their market. This is why communication means so much and has to be done right the first time around. To paraphrase the late Senator William Fulbright, great companies get into trouble and can go into long-term decline when they become arrogant in the use of their power and position, trying to do things that are not their core focus in places they shouldn't be.

I have worked with companies having similar technologies that rushed to market without fully knowing their competition. Timing becomes critical because existing competition indicates a market need and quick action should take place to fulfill the need. To strengthen the opportunity I have brought together companies with compatible technologies creating an integrated solution. Unfortunately, during their early stage most of the companies I spoke with were not interested in an alliance. They believed that they were different enough and could successfully go-to-market without enhancing their product.

These companies would prefer to copy each other rather than partner in the belief that they will take a leadership position in the market. Copying others tends to be a losing strategy in the long run. Alliances can create a stronger market position and greater chance for success.

The Tactics of Global Survival

All companies believe that they are close to their customers; they see a need, an opportunity, do a little market research and they are on their way. In fact, most entrepreneurs know very little about their customers. When reaching out to customers, many entrepreneurs describe what their product or service is and why their product is better than their competitors' and then explains to the customer why they should buy it. This is also how most salespeople make presentations. All too often in this process they leave out how the product can benefit the customer. The only time the customer is interested is when you can tell them how a product will improve their life.

Customers will often tell you what they want; few really know what they need. Those who understand what customers really need are in a better position to expand in the market and increase sales. Knowing what customers need is especially true when trying to sell products into foreign markets because the needs of those customers may not be the same as in your domestic market. If you haven't figured out how to grow in your domestic market, making an overseas foray is likely to be folly.

If the same failure statistics and reasoning holds true for those non-U.S. companies who want to enter the U.S. market, then ninety-five percent of all U.S. companies will fail who try to enter foreign markets. This is because entry costs on average are high, customer value is not presented or clearly defined and companies become focused on the process of setting up their company, offices and making contacts, not on revenue generation. The standard market entry approach fails because foreign companies are missing these critical pieces to the market entry puzzle:

- U.S. market information for their product

- Competitive intelligence about what is selling and whom they are up against

- Substantial capital that is required to set up offices, hire staff, and establish operations

- Limited U.S. strategic decision-making contacts

- Distribution and retail channels have not been established

- A trained local sales force to promote and sell the product

- The skills and knowledge needed to generate revenue

- Operational management support

- An understanding of the cultural business differences within the U.S.

- English language skills

For U.S. companies the order of foreign expansion is usually Canada, United Kingdom, Australia, the European Union, Japan, South Korea, China then the rest of the world. Normally this is the result of established trade relations, language, and available expertise to assist these companies.

Companies need to understand the dynamics of a specific country's market before going it alone. They will move forward selling their goods and services without understanding the new culture they are in. They try to duplicate their home country success abroad without the market and cultural knowledge needed. This cannot be gained overnight. Most are unaware of who the true customer is in this new market and how to create demand for the product. Not only do they not know their customer, but are unaware of supply chain and logistic factors needed to bring the product to market.

What is Needed to Enter a Foreign Market?

If you have an Internet site that is set-up for product sales and a secure payment method then you are already in the game. But in most cases this is not enough. It all begins with market research of the country, buying habits, disposable income, competitive products, regulation, tariffs and the import/export process established by these countries. But this type of market research does not effectively support the sales of your product. The questions you need to answer are:

- What does the ideal customer look like in terms of want and needs?

- What experts do you rely on to determine the best method of reaching these customers?

- What messages will resonate with the customer or specific channel or partner?

- What are the barriers to entry and how do you overcome them?

- What are the competitive challenges in entering a new market?

Foreign companies trying to enter the U.S. market should take their time in establishing a presence. The first goal should be to create product and company credibility and visibility through the establishment of references and market "buzz." This is more important than having a U.S. sales office. Most markets are based upon a network of influencers. These influencers could be experts in the field, press, analysts, bloggers, tweeters', celebrities, colleagues, customers, your business and social community, critics and trend setters. Not having an aligned strategy to build credibility and messaging with these people will reduce the chances of market-entry success. Distributors are more concerned with longevity, service and supply risks with foreign players than they are of missing out on a new and innovative product. Building credibility and trust become the key factors for growth and sustainability.

Because any new sales process can be very complex and time consuming, success takes persistence and dedication as well as individually tailored methods for every customer. Marketing can create demand in consumer products but not necessarily in business to business selling. Failure comes when you haven't figured out what the customer wants or needs and why or what they will buy. This was exemplified with the launch of Apple Inc.'s iPhone resulting in decreased sales of competitors' products such as Motorola and Nokia. Apple knew what customers wanted and delivered on it, which proves the point that alliances create success. Apple is the leader and the others are now chasing them.

To be visible you have to choose a message and a target audience. This can be accomplished by developing and maintaining ongoing relationships with the customer and building trust for your company and its products. The goal is to ensure that the distributor prefers to sell your product, such as AT&T, which has exclusivity to sell the iPhone. Do not expect distributors to add any value in the marketing and sales area because they are expecting you to bring the customers to them. It is critical that you understand how the potential prospects in each country perceive your product and how they communicate about it. It is said that Americans want to buy, but hate to be sold to. I believe this applies to all people around the world.

Knowing the Competition

Most executives believe they have superior products but generally lack in depth information about their competition. Most of these executives are surprised to discover the large number of competitors and the volume of sales in the industry when they expand worldwide. Many times management develops a new product or service that they believe is unique, has no competition and can be sold in limitless numbers. They forget that there may be a product or service that is fulfilling this need already. Few products on the market are truly new.

Customers have the opportunity to review numerous products from a variety of vendors but are limited by their available time. Your products are competing against a specific segment of products. Meaningful data on the central companies supplying these products, their size in terms of assets, sales, territory, years in business, location, distributors, and financial conditions becomes vital.

Product Pricing

Product price is an important variable due to the trend toward commoditization and labor arbitrage. Executives tend to believe that the competition sets the price and therefore the company has little control over what it can charge. Often companies find their competitors do not want to compete on price and try to avoid this form of competition. Retailers are getting tremendous sell-through at low price points and minimal margins. There is price resistance in certain product categories, which will increase as distributors change their product portfolio to respond to the market. In most cases executives do not know the range of prices in the market place and believe prices are far more important to the customer than is really the case. The price a company should charge for a product or service is production cost plus a fair profit.

Promotion

There are many means of promoting a product. Promotion is becoming more complex because of the many more specialized ways to reach existing and new customers. Almost all product areas have trade publications and trade shows directed toward a very specialized group of customers. Trade shows are an efficient means of reaching a large number of potential customers but on average very little business is finalized there. More business is transacted after hours at the hospitality suites than is done on the trade show floor. Trade shows provide the opportunity for showcasing your products while gathering names of prospective customers. With the decline in newspapers and the ever increasing use of the Web, concentration should be given to these new social and business Internet communities because the demographics of the new buying power rests with those 40 years old and younger who are increasing their usage of the Internet.

Distribution

Traditional distribution systems are changing rapidly due to streamlined methods making short production runs economical and manageable. To do this on an international basis requires a focus on increasing quality awareness, an extensive communication network and just-in-time production. Just-in-time delivery, where little or no inventory is being carried has expanded worldwide and is causing the supply chain to reconsider how it performs its operation. This will have the biggest impact on exporters in Asia who expect importers at trade shows to purchase their products for importation. This effective way of doing business is changing as importers today want to assume less risk. Those systems that were effective only a few years ago may no longer be effective. Foreign companies must re-evaluate their distribution systems to ensure that they can respond to a customer as quickly as local companies.

Opportunity Trends

Anticipating sales trends industry-wide are essential in preparing a market entry plan. The market entry plan will leverage this information and will build a solid picture of the product's potential in the targeted market. The products' uniqueness or its differentiators from other comparable products become important. In the long run the goal is to either be a top five company in your market space or in a position to be acquired by another company. Because the universality of the Internet can make the buyer much more knowledgeable and savvier than a supplier, having a solid plan will help to differentiate your product from the others. Information about the firm's home country sales and total projected sales volume can be used to forecast sales in a foreign market. The opportunity for a foreign company depends upon the stages in the product's life cycle. The options that are available to the company will vary by the goals of executive management. In many cases to avoid head-on competition it is best to find other solutions for the product to generate revenue for the company. The enterprise sales model for most businesses striving for international expansion will have to find new sales analysis and market entry methods due to the complexity of:

- Economic conditions in the targeted market

- Customer demand

- Logistics required to go-to-market

- Start-up and operational cost issues

Sales teams at small companies often are outmanned and outspent by larger competitors. But even the large competitors have lost sales because they didn't do their homework. This happened when Safeway Inc. choose to promote Challah, a traditional Jewish egg bread, during the holiday of Passover. If the bakery merchandisers had taken the time to understand the rituals of the holiday they would have realized that bread is not eaten during this holiday, only Matzo. So the only customers buying the Challah were those not observing Passover. Many cultural rituals are misunderstood, which can lead to lost sales because the merchandisers lack the information about their customer base. If they had known their customers they would have increased sales instead of losing them.

Whether it is perks offered or simply more staff, big business seems to have the advantage in getting new customers. You have to get customers to buy in along the way to be in a position to close the deal. For most of the last two decades products and services seemed to sell themselves as a booming global economy made businesses spenders as they positioned themselves for growth.

Salespeople believe that they can close any deal because it is hard to disqualify someone you are in communications with. The cost of customer acquisition is the driving factor for revenue generation and profitability in any market. Every sales representative's goal is to sell to the highest executive in their target companies. In many cases this may not be the decision maker. Many product-buying decisions, whether for consumer goods or technology products, are made at lower levels in a company. Knowing who to leverage and how buying decisions are made is imperative. The key is to find the strategic influencers in the organizations and have them sell your product to their company. Most people don't like to do cold calls whether they are Americans or not and most don't want to disqualify a prospect. Successful companies always measure their results, whether it is a sales plan or marketing program to determine if these investments provide a measurable return. If you can't measure it, don't do it!

Customers

The first step in entering a new market is to focus on creating a sustainable pipeline for more business, not just leads or potential distributors or partners. What is required are fewer high quality leads that have a serious desire of beginning the sales process. This should begin prior to even stepping off the plane in a foreign market. It is important to develop key criteria in terms of time, costs, and the prospective turnover rate. Use your established social and business communities or hire a reputable market entry firm to help cultivate your potential customers prior to spending thousands of dollars relocating staff to the foreign country.

Supporting the sales process is the primary goal for all companies. I was once asked by a principal account manager in Switzerland for a Silicon Valley computer firm to travel to Geneva on short notice for a one hour meeting with a prominent client. The flight time was twelve hours each way and the cost for the flight, room, and expenses were disproportionate for a one hour meeting. The idea of doing a video conference was presented to the client who was in favor of the idea. The client was so impressed with the video conferencing facilities and our concern for not wasting time or money it convinced him to use our services. You never know what the customer wants until you ask, but you have to take the chance that what you decide is what they will want.

By developing virtual communities you can use the members to not only become lead-generation candidates but to become your virtual sales force. This will provide you with an edge over other companies in your same industry. Communities form and grow around valuable information. Unfortunately customer turnover is frequently very high and management generally does not analyze this turnover. Network savvy companies may be able to find out why customers cease to buy products by directly asking their network. Many executives monitor their networks for negative information about their company and can respond to a negative blog or tweet within minutes helping to solve the problem and establishing a relationship with the customer. I have found that market entry research, even though time consuming provides the basis for accurate and realistic decision making. Most CEOs of successful companies make it a matter of policy to visit with their key customers on a regular basis.

Demand

Executives understand that one company that is well positioned can influence their competition and the demand for a product. Marketers know that if the desire can be created to own a product there will be those customers who are willing to pay for it. Savvy manufacturers know that the amount of product being manufactured will have an impact on demand and on the price. Usually when the price increases the demand will decrease.

If your competitor hopes to gain a larger market share by reducing his prices thus creating demand this will put you in a difficult position. You will either have to reduce your prices or lose sales. If the demand for the product is greater than the supply, substitute products will be used by the consumer to compensate. Just because the customer has the money to purchase your product doesn't always mean they will. As with large screen TVs and other electronics, people will wait for the prices to drop rather than pay full price just to be the first to own one. Only if a consumer believes that the price of the product will be higher in the future will he be more likely to purchase it now.

If you lower your prices in the belief that you will create demand remember other companies tend to follow the leader and will reduce their prices also. The best example of this is the grocery industry where if one grocer reduces their prices the others will usually follow. As a result, total sales will only increase slightly, but will be at a lower price. Larger companies with buying power and additional resources will have the advantage in this regard whether they are a Wal-Mart selling similar products or your main competitor. These companies will put pressure on you to match their pricing and support structure thus forcing you to reduce your prices and your margins. Their demand will stay high but yours may decrease. If you don't have flexibility in your operations and pricing structure your competitor will be in a position to force you out of business. Market analysis will show why you should be concerned about promotion and quality rather than the price of the product. Prices are used in promotion when companies really do not understand demand.

Quality Requirements

Companies have rediscovered the importance of quality, which they now see as a competitive factor. Quality improvement is not a fad, but a long-term, continuous effort. A company's quality program is an important part of the marketing plan and should become a competitive part of your company's strategy. Without the consideration of quality you can end up with lead in toys or poisonous chemicals in pet food. These types of situations can be disastrous for a company or even an entire country. With the present emphasis on quality in the U.S. a company must stress this in their marketing plan.

Going Green

In today's environmentally conscience societies, this issue must be an important consideration in any market entry program as well as advertising and promotion. Safe environmental practices can be presented as a favorable image to the market and can enhance the firm's marketing and sales efforts especially for that demographic most concerned about the environment and "green technology."

Natural "green" products that can be recycled are user-friendly and employ sustainable materials that do not contain hazardous elements are now considered imperative in many cultures and differentiates the product. Are there hazardous elements that have to be published on the labels? Do they require special disposal? Many countries now have policies for recycling of both the products and packaging. This can be voluntary or in many cases it is a buy-back policy with the design of products and packaging using materials that can be recycled such as glass and aluminum.

Consumers are interested in green products and products that will last. Many of the products imported into America have planned obsolesce built into them and are not designed to last. When you see a product that has been in use for a long period of time, the question is why can't today's products be engineered to last as long. There is an incandescent light bulb made by the Shelby Electric Company installed at a fire department in Livermore, California in 1901. For 109 years this light bulb has been in continuous use. If only they made the same quality energy efficient light bulbs today that would last even half that time.

5 The Challenges of the U.S. Market

By prevailing over all obstacles and distractions, one may unfailingly arrive at his chosen goal or destination.
Christopher Columbus

Albert Einstein once commented, "imagination is more important than knowledge." Einstein could not have conceived his many theories without imagination just as entrepreneurs need imagination to create new and exciting products. Innovation and risk taking has propelled the United States to dominate the world market leaving the old world behind to wonder what it will take to develop a new breed of entrepreneur.

Various industry executives from around the world make the pilgrimage to Silicon Valley and other cities in the U.S. to meet with their counterparts to determine if their products will be accepted by these U.S. companies. Some will be seeking sales and distributions channels, others will attend trade shows, and many will attend corporate briefings. Some will trek to Silicon Valley going from one venture capitalist to another furnishing them with cookie cutter executive summaries, business plans, and boring PowerPoint presentations just to brief these money men on how their technology will revolutionize the world if only they would first provide them funding. Then there are the government delegates from China, Vietnam, Malaysia, and other countries that come looking for American foreign direct investment to help their countries' industries grow. But only a handful will seriously look to establish a presence in the United States.

The companies that make the trek are considered by their home country to be the "pearls" of opportunity—the best of the best. Unlike VCs, these entrepreneurs haven't had the advantage of evaluating thousands of similar business plans and are not usually aware of what other companies are doing in comparison. After gracefully being rejected by the VCs, they return home empty handed. Competition in Silicon Valley is cutthroat, and less than one percent of business plans receive venture capital funding. This reinforces that the barriers to entry for new companies are high. It also shows that in more sophisticated markets it is harder to get funding for technology that cannot be differentiated or supported. The executive that doesn't navigate these challenges carefully runs the risk of being disregarded by the funding community.

Globalization does not mean that all products will become the same worldwide; it does means that companies will maintain their own identity, culture and distinctiveness thereby providing innovation in their home market with the expectation for global expansion. This is best exemplified by Wal-Mart with its 3,700 stores worldwide. Wal-Mart uses its name on many of its stores but it also uses some sixty other names acquired in their pursuit of new markets in different parts of the world. Wal-Mart learned that the American way doesn't always win new markets. In the past they have failed to gain market share using the superstore format with products unfamiliar to the local population. Wal-Mart and similar companies are pioneering innovative products and new store formats in numerous countries. This involves taking new and different products and ideas from around the world and transplanting them to locations with customers who are open and accepting of innovation.

Today I find many non-U.S. corporate executives who consider a focus on creativity to be a waste of time, an exercise that doesn't have the quick ROI. U.S. companies derive their strength from the all-American spirit of competition with a balance of cooperation and the infusion of creativity. U.S. companies and the venture capital community watch for these creative companies that have a potential for large payoffs at low costs.

Watching Hollywood movies or television programs like "Dallas" or "Friends" doesn't really make you knowledgeable of American culture or how business is conducted. Visiting the country as a tourist or even going to an American university will only provide a small glimpse of the vast diversity of the nation. Because of the American media influence in products worldwide, foreign executives may believe they know the American market and feel confident introducing their products. I have met many executives who believe they know American tastes and buying habits. But without research and proper preparation these companies are likely to fail no matter how excellent their product. The failure rate for new American businesses is approximately 75% in the first year alone with only about half of those who survive the first year remaining in business for the next five years. Sad to say, these are businesses that should know their customers and not become over confident in their assessment of their opportunity. Given these odds, what chance does a foreign company have in the U.S. market? While a listing of reasons for business failures would at first seem lengthy the majority of the causes can be condensed down to money, management, and marketing. But these can all be overcome with proper preparation.

The Silicon Valley success model that brings innovative ideas through to a final product is based on individual imagination followed by willing-ness to assume risk. Americans have repeatedly proven that they are willing to assume the risk and have built some of the most successful companies in history. On the other hand, I see many executives from Western Europe, Latin America and Southeast Asia who only want to assume minimal risk. Out of necessity foreign companies need to expand but their executives tend to be hesitant when faced with the possibility of moving away from the comfort zone of their local market and culture. When provided with new models of revenue generation they prefer to fall back on what has been successful for them.

Such as the case of a Chinese firm who had the opportunity to sell their products online but because of their business traditions the company refused to try the online method and insisted their products be bought outright and warehoused. Being risk adverse they did not wish to sell on consignment. This proved to be a deal breaker for the U.S. online distributor. The Chinese firm didn't understand that this is the way the distributor wanted to do business. A small to medium sized company can manufacture for their local market but when asked to manufacture on a larger scale this may present financial difficulties. Capital may become an issue when trying to enter a larger market. On the positive side, this hesitancy encourages planning, builds confidence and can minimize the risk. It also may mean that they will not take any action. They tend to develop "analysis paralysis" and decide to postpone the decision to a later date.

The problem is that competition can come from any corner of the world and being hesitant to expand outside of your home market may lead to your own failure. International companies who have entered your country's market obviously aren't hesitant.

The Survival of the Global Emerging Company

The most important prerequisite for survival and growth is to find the country in which there is an environment where achievement and wealth creation is held in high esteem. When this is the case there exists the regulatory and tax environment that doesn't hinder new companies and will reward risk takers. America continues to have the world's largest influx of foreign direct investment. For over two centuries individuals, companies, and governments have bought land, factories, real estate, and other commercial assets. The United States may rank third according to the World Bank after Singapore and New Zealand for the ease of doing business, but foreign companies want to establish themselves in the U.S. because there is greater market potential and world influence.

There are only a handful of nations where the general populous appears to embrace an entrepreneurial spirit and a global trade culture. These include Israel, Canada, Brazil, Denmark, South Korea, Hong Kong, and others that stand out among many of the nations for their achievements. To the advantage of those living in America, the majority of companies in those countries are not likely in the foreseeable future to change their attitude toward entrepreneurship and bi-lateral trade.

Local companies may have greater influence and stronger relationships to local suppliers, which may in the long run allow them to buy at lower prices. Foreign companies entering a new market are at a disadvantage not knowing the cultural subtleties of a region and how it applies to merchandising and selling a product. That is why sending a trusted friend or family member into a new market to build the business for you does not always work. Knowing the basics of selling in one country doesn't always lend itself to selling in another.

When selling an idea the first stage is pre-market development. The product is in incubation or early stage design when a company is developing user specifications, influencing thought leaders, or determining market requirements. The second stage is post market when you have a finalized product.

An Israeli delegation of wireless company executives came to Silicon Valley to meet their American counterparts. In preparation for their meetings I presented each company's technology to its targeted U.S. counterpart to determine whether it would be worthwhile for them to meet face-to-face. On the day of the meetings I was surprised when one of the Israeli companies presented an entirely new array of technologies and products to the Americans. What the Israeli company forgot was that these U.S. companies had a focused interest in the product ideas and were looking forward to discussing these with the Israeli representatives. So as not to lose the opportunity for the Israeli company we did spin control to help them get back on track. Their presentation now went beyond their original product line to show the progression of innovative technologies that were available. Damage control was done. The American CEOs were impressed with the amount of innovation coming from these companies. The Israelis took the risk and they won.

This is generally not the case because venture capitalists have limited time and patience. You need knowledgeable people in the target market to help and assist you; otherwise you are setting yourself up for failure.

Marketing involves far more than just knowing a market and what motivates consumers. Most businesses focus on the marketing "push," but few ever focus on the "pull," which is one of the secrets to success. The "push" puts product into the distribution channel or inventory on a retailer's shelves, because you are pushing products through your pipeline and realizing sales at your end. What you want is the "pull" when customers want your product. It is your responsibility, not that of the dealer, to make potential customers aware of what your product is and will do for them. This can be done in many ways especially through the use of social media that you have developed along with traditional PR and marketing.

Market feedback is one reason that the U.S. has so many innovative entrepreneurs and companies. The goal is to think through what you currently bring to the table and to get a better sense of the type of resources you will need to commit to your business for the future. Following industry trends can move the company toward better performance, provided that the data is up-to-date and the company and its employees have the ability to act on it. You can accomplish this by:

- Collecting trend information through focused data from market entry research

- Developing models using the market research data through beta testing and other available means

- Practice "what if analysis," which can help determine the best course of action under various scenarios

- Having the flexibility to act on insight and assumptions and to adopt the research results into the products or programs

Determining business trends and knowing the likelihood of events occurring is of no use unless the entrepreneur has the flexibility to adapt and take action. By doing so, this process also provides the benefit of inspiring a sense of urgency about the future.

New strategies derived from this type of business planning have the potential to create distinct competitive advantages. By highlighting warning signs such as a competitor's product being demonstrated at a trade show, a negative article in the *Wall Street Journal*, or a drop in stock price a business can avoid surprises and be better prepared to adapt and act effectively. You should be able to answer the following questions.

- Who will be your customers in three to five years?

- What channels will be used to reach them?

- Are traditional channels currently serving the company's needs?

- Are your short-term priorities aligned with your long-term goals?

- What constitutes your competitive advantage?

- Are you aware of new competitive threats either in the States or abroad?

- Is change driven by your competitors' actions or by your own unique vision of the future?

I have asked these types of questions to hundreds of companies over the years with few executives having definite answers or who have taken the time to do their due diligence of the market.

I once was dealing with a successful real estate entrepreneur who made his millions developing properties across the United States. Through his networking and contacts he was awarded exclusive rights for the commercial use of a technology that was developed and used by the U.S. government. He was not looking for funding but for a partner who would help him take his new product to industry segments that he was unfamiliar with. Not knowing technology, he wanted us to determine what changes we thought would be required for the product to be ready for the market and what industries he should go after. After working with him over time it became apparent that he was unable to go beyond his background and to approach this opportunity in a new light. He was unsuccessful in answering these key questions for the business. In the end, he returned the license back to the government.

It's All About Results!

Innovation and creativity make business more competitive through efficiency in operations, which increases productivity and reduces costs. It will also help you to expand globally to increase revenue and market share. Innovation is not your traditional problem solving, it is the process of creating new and different products that people wait in line to buy. Think iPhone, Wii, or Amazon's Kindle.

So what do highly innovative companies have in common? The foundation for creative thinking is an open system for experimentation, dialogue, and for challenging assumptions and testing results. This should be done prior to sending your representative to the new country, doing so will save you time and money. Participation in this process should include employees, suppliers, partners and customers who don't have preconceived notions of how things should be done. Usually they can be trusted to come up with challenging new ideas.

Innovation can be used both to increase the profitability of companies by either internal development as well as through the merger and acquisition process. Look back at history to the American industrial revolution with its captains of industry. These capitalists met on a regular basis to keep each other informed of their various enterprises. The railroad tycoon informed the steel and real estate tycoons of opportunities that were advantageous to them all. This increased their wealth until the government eventually intervened to limit their control. Controlling innovation development we find that markets can also be controlled, but only for a limited amount of time.

The fate of corporations lies in the understanding that long-term damage comes not from foreign competition, but often is self-inflicted. Countries whose leaders, businesses, and citizens are not driven by success or innovation and are slow to respond to the everyday changes occurring around them are unlikely to respond to the greater challenges that they now face with globalization. Governmental agencies try to assist their home companies to enter new markets, but their goals and the goals of private business are different. Government agencies have measurable goals; how many trips can be logged, how many speeches presented, and how many companies can be persuaded to attend the event being sponsored. Most governments are not innovative or creative. They can make introductions or provide real estate but cannot guide a business to effectively enter a new market and be profitable. Governmental agencies and organizations like the chambers of commerce can be helpful in determining the sources of power that can affect your business and its ability to take hold in a new market. Their role is not to help generate sales and create revenue for you.

The Market Makers

Going after the key influencers in the private market is critical. There is nothing like a reference account in your new market to increase your creditability. If it happens to be in a vertical industry that others look to as a leader, all the better. An article written about your company and products in a leading publication, on TV, or an influential blog may change the course of your company. A successful implementation or a beta test for a crucial account can effectively influence the direction of an industry and propel your company to new heights. Other companies tend to follow market leaders and having a foothold in a prime industry account can make that difference.

Key influencers may have you perform at your own expense to get your beta to trial at their facility. Establishing up-front what will be a reasonable performance criteria and expectations in time, resources, and service will be necessary. Both parties need to be flexible enough to acknowledge that over time the agreement will be modified.

Insights into the challenges these companies are facing in growing sales revenues, retaining existing customers and attracting new ones in the current economic climate will add value to your offering.

When contemplating entering a new market the main question to answer is if the product is relevant to the market. Wal-Mart quickly found out that selling golf clubs in their South American stores did not go over well. There was little interest by the consumer. The real difference between the survivors and those who are going to fail in any market is focusing on the customers' needs. In addition to your product being relevant, you may have to change your positioning tactics depending on how your business customer uses your product to improve their bottom line. Jack Welch, the former CEO of General Electric overstated when he commented that the only position in the market is being number one. You do not have to be number one in a market to be profitable. Often it is better to be in the position of the underdog because there is less pressure on you and your company to maintain your numbers constantly.

Proving to a customer that you have the best product or return on investment will not always secure the deal. At some point in the negotiations, the customer will ask how you intend to support their account. If you are a foreign start-up, just entering the market the problem may become a deal breaker. The customer will require assurances that you will have the support staff available and the spare parts on hand necessary to support them. Service also applies to having additional product on-hand to fulfill orders within a limited time. This applies to in demand consumer products especially during the holiday season. Customers will bring up many issues before you even get to the ROI issue. It is not just ROI; it is the reduction of their risk with a new and foreign company. They need to know that you will be there for them a year from now.

The Marketing Mix

Every company operates with the same four elements of the marketing mix. These are often referred to as the "four Ps." These four elements remain constant but the emphasis on the resources devoted to each will vary depending on your individual business.

- **Product** - Successful companies are those who consider their marketing and customer needs even at the very earliest stages of market entry development.

- **Price** - The need is to determine what price point that delivers a profit customers can afford to pay and is competitive with others who are selling a similar product.

- **Place** - The place customers can actually purchase the product. This can include retail stores, wholesale, online, or other distribution means.

- **Promotion** - Activities designed to inform customers about what is offered and encourages them to buy.

To get this mix right requires an understanding of the needs, motivations, and buying process of the customer. Consider the benefits of buying your product from the customers' perspective and what your competitors are doing to foil your plans. Then determine what makes you stand apart from them. Putting this together in terms of customer benefit, not just the technology will assist in developing an exceptional selling proposition.

In pursuing business opportunities in a foreign country the ideal situation would be to seal a partnership or customer agreement and then set up an office to service the client and to expand your business. A company should always appear local even if they are not. This means a local address, phone number, URL, Web site, etc. Even if you plan to use agents for the near future you will need to get these details right. Having a local presence either with an agent or with your own staff provides easier access to the target market. This way a sales call no longer means an overseas business trip. Even with the Internet and the use of social media, face-to-face business meetings are still important in establishing trust. Having local "feet on the ground" provides less perceived risk for your clients and partners while providing firsthand inside information about what is occurring in the market.

I know of a Japanese company who hired a president of U.S. operations to help them in opening the American market for their product. The new president was a recent engineering graduate from an American university here on a student visa. He did not know the first thing about developing channels or how to set up a company. On top of this, he is Chinese and his native tongue is Mandarin, which made his accented English difficult to understand. It was apparent from the beginning this was a very foolish business decision on the part of the Japanese company. Not only was this individual inexperienced for the task, but because of a change in his visa status he had to return to China. The Japanese company then reconsidered their objective and decided not to enter the U.S.

The Japanese company should have started by using outsourced representation, which would have saved them a substantial financial and time commitment and provided knowledgeable resources right from the beginning. Doing so would realistically have saved them a minimum of $250,000, which they spent covering their first year operating costs. This amount did not including marketing and business development. The Japanese company did little if any research in order to ensure that they would be able to generate a return on their investment. It took them double the time to ramp up their U.S. operations. Normally in the first six months, the executive's time is devoted to establishing an office and not generating sales.

What they could have done because they were not ready to set-up a full overseas office was to create the appearance of a local office. They could have done this without leaving home. The first step is to have a high quality Web site and URL in the target country's language. The Web site has to be inviting and clearly present your company's products and its history. The message should be short, to the point, and require an action to motivate people to contact you. A prospects' first contact with your company may be through your Web site. You will need to work with someone inside the country to assist with the translation and layout even though you may know the language and culture.

It is extremely helpful to have a local e-mail account and a local phone number. To manage the time zone differences it would be advisable to have voicemail that states that you will return their call within a specified period. Video conferencing can be an excellent way to communicate with partners and other teams who are working closely with your company. There are also service firms that can forward mail and act as a receptionist service during business hours for a monthly fee. You should be aware however, that in some countries it might be necessary to comply with local laws if you are operating with a foreign address even if you are not physically present.

The quickest way to enter a new market is with agents, resellers, distributors, and others who are focused on opening new territories. Fortunately, agent and reseller recruitment takes less time than building a direct sales team. Taking the time to pick and vet the best agents and distributors who are targeted on your customer base will save time and money in the end. Research those distributors who focus on your specialty and if it is a match for your company's need. Using the right agent to evaluated and negotiate contracts with distributors can cut the startup time up to three months. Many large distributors require that you use their template, which in turn will save you time and money.

Market development funds (MDF), which are used to help sell or market your products, may be required by the distributor. The money required may be a fixed amount usually in the range of $50,000 (USD) or based on a percentage (1% to 2%) that will be agreed to as part of an overall marketing plan. Typical advertising campaigns will run for a period of six months and average about $15,000 to $20,000 per month.

Retailers may require that foreign products be shipped in approved packaging with barcodes and security devices attached. They may also request size specific packaging to fit their shelves as well as the carton holders for J-Hooks. Prior to designing the packaging, it is advisable to check what written information is required by law.

Your channels are unconcerned as to whether you use contracted or permanent staff. They are more concerned about the overall experience level within the company and the level of demand generation programs that are planned. They expect to see a thoughtful marketing plan to create pull and adequate funds behind the plan to assure its success. Reference accounts as well as product run rate information is often required and will help speed the acceptance process. The more you can work together with your distributors the greater the chances of success.

In economic hard times, new companies offering consumer goods may have to consign their products to a distributor just to get into the market. Retailers are hesitant to mark down products and take a loss. Therefore, they push down the risk to the distributor or the supplier. The positive side of doing business this way is the manufacturer can have better control of inventory. The downside of using consignment is that payment will not occur until the distributor sells the product and collects their money. A credit card purchase by a customer can result in payment to the supplier taking up to ninety days after the sale depending on their return policy. Channel partners will only provide support for as long as there remains a joint sales commitment and immediate revenue for both parties. It is advisable, therefore, to develop multiple channels where revenues can be increased.

Selecting the right channel will vary according to your product or service. Companies with products aimed at particular niche industries such as automotive or financial services should look at geographic trends in that vertical industry and select the channel in the most appropriate area. Until recently, most of the U.S. automotive industry was located in the mid-west, from Illinois to Pennsylvania with its heart being in Detroit. On the other hand, the banking and insurance industries are located in the Northeast except for a few pockets in San Francisco, Chicago, and North Carolina. A good approach would be to select one or two likely candidates and then thoroughly research their sales potential and their competition, which could affect your success. The information you will need to determine your target market may include some of the following considerations.

- How quickly do the suppliers' customers accept new technologies?

- What are the technological standards or lack of that will affect your product?

- How sophisticated are the targeted end users?

- Is the required infrastructure in place to support your product?

- How regulated is the industry in the targeted country?

Vertical industry marketing may mean that the product, partners, messages, and sales cycle might require focused changes to be in line with the industry. The value proposition for the product has to be focused on the industry and a specific clientele. Moving from a horizontal value proposition to a vertical industry based one can take over a year in a large market to yield that type of revenue needed to sustain operations.

As a product matures, it may facilitate infrastructure growth required to support that technology. This in turn may become a business in itself or a service offering. A good example of this is Apple Computer's iPhone. A whole industry has grown up around supplying applications (Apps) for the phone. When you add video to the phone it behooves companies such as AT&T to advance their internal infrastructure to make sure that the bandwidth required is available to provide the needed services to their customers. With the launch of the Nexus One smart phone, Google has initiated a new business and distribution model using carriers to offer wireless plans through their Web site. The carriers may have to change their infrastructure to support the new Google applications.

Consider areas that will have a greater impact on the successful implementation of a product or service. Look for those that may require infrastructure changes, higher product adoption rates, economic health and activity, greater market stability. As an example, the trend has moved away from Detroit to foreign automobile companies who are locating their U.S. manufacturing facilities to the Southeast portion of the country. If these companies are your target market, maybe you should be there too.

When refining the market for your products there may be additional factors for you to consider. These may be the income level of your preferred customer, their sophistication in using new technologies, the population, location, buying patterns, and the level of competitive activity initiated by your competition.

Regulation and legislation relevant to your technology will affect how you adjust your marketing strategy and sales process. This is particularly relevant for biotech, pharmaceutical and medical device companies but increasingly Internet and other IT product companies are being affected by and prosecuted under local privacy, censorship, and copyright laws.

If you are doing business overseas the nature of the banking system as well as foreign exchange rates, methods of payment, record keeping, tariffs, and price controls all become factors in determining your profitability.

Depending if it is the relocation of corporate headquarters, a U.S. subsidiary or just establishing a sales office, there are many issues to deal with in a physical move. The first issue to be handled is the best place to establish an office. Each region of the U.S. is distinctive and so are the cities located there. Real estate prices vary by location. Where would your customers be? Do you need access to a major international airport? Wal-Mart Stores, the world's largest public corporation by revenue has its corporate headquarters in Bentonville, Arkansas that had a population in 2007 of 33,744. Many U.S. and international companies have a presence there even though the city is small compared to others in the state and nation. Relocation, office setup, and manufacturing facilities all vary depending on what is required to support your operations. The other issues are transportation, education, and facilities to name a few.

Finding the Right People

Staff recruitment will probably be the single most important issue you will face when expanding your overseas presence. It is important to get local talent, as they will have experience in the market and more importantly a network of contacts that your home country staff cannot supply. Hiring local staff can be more expensive and time consuming but the investment is worthwhile if you know the culture, law, and the best ways to motivate your recruits. Many foreign companies will outsource this initial function to a representative in the target country who will assist you in the hiring process. Outsourcing to the right companies can create faster demand and sales and prove the viability of the product in the market. There are other types of hiring firms that will find you key employees that complement your team. These individuals would initially work for stock options or other types of incentives.

Search firms usually specialize in one kind of search such as Chief Financial Offers, Vice Presidents and technical staff and they usually require a sum equal to the first year's pay for this individual. These placement firms will help write a job description and then provide resumes of people that meet your specifications. If you have developed an international online community, you can get references and suggestions of which recruiters are the best by industry and locations and are available to assist.

The goal is to be one of the top three companies in your industry space. To do this will require you to network at an executive level and to understand the local politics and planning in the competitor's organization. Networking is the best way to meet potential high-level employees. By networking, you can meet prospective employees, determine what their contribution could be to your company, and gather intelligence about your competitors. Be aware of cultural differences in that some people do not tend to state their achievements as strongly as others do.

In addition to salary, executive personnel frequently benefit from stock option plans, performance bonuses, and other non-salary benefits. Get an idea of the correct payment levels by talking to contacts in similar roles or by using salary surveys and other reports.

In the U.S. and European market, you should examine the state and federal labor laws to get an indication of your obligations as an employer. It is important that all employees are legally entitled to work in their respective markets and that they can produce appropriate identifications and papers as required. It is often advisable to have a local human resource consultant help you to establish your company's policies and procedures.

As markets slow down and there are more people looking for jobs remember it is still a relatively tight labor market for qualified people. Candidates can be skeptical about joining an unknown business from a foreign country. They are worried about management style, whether the company will be around tomorrow and even whether the option program is legitimate. It is not easy coming into a new market and getting the best talent. That is why outsourcing makes great sense.

Many people have come from other countries that you may want to hire. These candidates may not be the best fit for your business if the primary goal is sales, business and market development. The mistake that most companies make entering a foreign market is to bring their own staff. Just because they were successful in their home market does not mean they understand the challenges associated with entering and working in a foreign market.

6 Market Entry Options

It helps to fish where the fish are.
Unknown

A foreign market provides a new array of entry options for the business executive. The options available fall into two distinct categories. The first are alliance options, which range from the tactical to strategic. The second are sales and marketing, which are based on the longevity of the relationship. These options can be further broken down by geography, demographics or vertical industry segmentation.

After numerous meetings and discussions with foreign trade commissioners and executives from the chambers of commerce, I noticed a lack of knowledge that impeded their assisting their compatriots, due to their unfamiliarity with the intricacies of the U.S. market. For some making introductions and collecting fees is their main concern while others will go beyond that to provide office space and mentoring. Neither of these is enough to be of any value. Making introductions is a good first step but falls short in building a sustainable business. One particular foreign trade officer was so unfamiliar with the basics that I had to educate him on U.S. Market Entry 101, which includes:

- The competitive landscape

- U.S. industry trends

- Direct industry competition

- Sales and distribution channels

- Available alliances and partnerships

- Management and operations

Foreign companies also have to consider the kinds of support and training that would be required to build these partnerships. Companies such as IBM, Cisco Systems, and Hewitt Packard lead their sales efforts by first introducing services. Foreign companies need to consider this model and integrate it into their market entry plan.

There is a broad range of options available depending on whether a company's objectives for market entry are additional contracts, a merger or acquisition, alliances, or venture capital funding. In every country some or all of these options exist but the U.S. market is a good example of the diversity of options from which a company trying to enter a new market can choose.

Those companies aware and open to exploring these options also need enablers for success in the market. These are:

1. **Product leadership**—a product that will stand out and fulfill a need

2. **Operational excellence**—efficiency in operations and excellent service

3. **Customer intimacy**—knowledge of the customer, and dedication to satisfying their needs

It requires a lot of time and effort to be the best at any of the three let alone all of them. In reality you only need two out of the three for success. However, if there is fear or doubt about managing a business in a new market, unlimited finances will not make a difference. Previous success may not be relevant when executives are reviewed on results. The exorbitant pressure to have an immediate return on investment on top of any additional pressures internally may hinder success.

When a company first comes into the American market they either want to do direct sales on their own or will focus on distributors or representatives to handle the bulk of the business for them. Many high technology companies take the approach of going it alone, relocating a staff member (usually sales) or the CEO over to the United States who will either rent their own office space or co-locate in specially designed centers that provide space and infrastructure for domestic and foreign companies. Having a presence in the market provides first-hand intelligence and direct access to prospective customers. Unfortunately the learning curve is extremely high and the timeframe is long before you can recover the cost of your operations. Using these centers usually means staying in your comfort zone and not getting out to your target customers. Whether you use a country-sponsored center or a private one, this method of entry has a high probability for failure.

Choosing the Right Distribution Channel

The U.S., unlike other countries, offers foreign companies a large, easy-to-access marketplace with a limited number of restrictions. Entry becomes easier and the probability for success increases if the right method of distribution is selected. Growth is the goal for most companies that desire a worldwide reach. They need to prepare by setting up international operations and selecting the right distribution channel and partners. When most companies decide they need to broaden their scope they look for partners that have the technical and financial capability to support their product and the right distribution channels to reach their target customers and grow.

I have seen countless business plans that commit to growing their business through partnerships but in reality it never materializes. All companies are primarily concerned about their own livelihood and will concentrate their efforts on what will bring in revenue for the short term to stay in business. This is no different in a partnership. By identifying a select group of partners who are capable of supporting your specific program objectives you can begin to determine if these selected partners are readily available for you and not promoting a competitor's product. With business networking, both you and the channels have the ability to find information and get feedback on any company anywhere in the world.

Entry to the U.S market can be done by means of Internet access, sales representatives, distributors, licensees, OEMs, or VARs. These approaches are not mutually exclusive and can be done in tandem. As an emerging company you do not have that many advantages in a new market and in most cases the large multinational companies tend not to view you as competition. The more a product is different and increases value through awareness, the more likely it is to reach the channels. The more you can reach your targeted customers the better. This is where using social media becomes important to increase demand.

Customers today are very nervous about buying products and services through untried companies whether foreign or domestic. If you have established an Internet following for your products before entry, this momentum will provide you with broader channels and faster market acceptance and the ultimate reference account—customers. By analyzing every step in your prospective partners supply chain and production process you can help them take out waste and costs. In retail, any brand that can no longer pull its weight will be evaluated before it sits too long on valuable shelf space.

The complexity of the product will determine which types of market entry methods would be best to pursue. The first step would be to carefully evaluate your company's objectives in the targeted market and plan a program that is geared towards meeting those objectives. Factors to include in your company's market entry program are:

- State and local incentives including investment tax credits, foreign trade zone benefits, discounted real estate, free training dollars, tax financing as well as others.

- Benefits of the product to the channel including any training required, the best local representation to use, what information is available to access the existing customer base to up-sell the product, demonstration products, discounted pricing models available by industry, free product samples, technical support and assistance needed as well as industry focused sales literature.

- The types of marketing materials required whether literature, CDs, Web sites, webinars, collateral and other materials should be professionally and locally developed and include materials and literature for each of your products. Your VARS will need these in order to promote your products to their clients.

- The channel and distribution partners needed to cover your industry segment, region of the country, customers supplied, the manufacturer's line of products carried, the margins they expect, and their sales incentive programs.

- Sales plan to include specific quarterly buy-in and sell-through targets, budgets, operational and support requirements. This should be in enough detail that future performance measurements can be based on these criteria for effective company management.

- Written reseller and channel agreement templates and authorization agreements should be developed by local legal representatives who will outline the terms, rights of the dealer, dealer obligations, license to use your logos and trademarks, ownership of proprietary rights and non-disclosure, warranty, termination, and any exclusivity rights. The channel partner may request that you use theirs but even so it is good to have developed your own to know the areas that you may wish to negotiate.

The key to building successful alliances is to ensure that the time and resources spent finding partners are a strategic fit for your product and can provide mutual benefit. Prospective partners will base their agreements on your commitment to the market, which will require you to perform due diligence on their product portfolio and customer base. By looking at their previous experience and record of accomplishment gives a basic indicator of their methodology and success factors. Conduct due diligence on the partnership using resources such as Bloomberg, Lexus-Nexus, and company 10K reports. The information should include revenue reports, the number of customers and their demographics, lead qualification, reference accounts, the agreement structure, and whether MDF funds are required.

Foreign manufactures wishing to enter a new market should have a thought out reseller and distributor program ready before approaching any potential channel partner. The better prepared the greater chance of success. More than likely you will need to provide on-site training for any new channel partners. If your resellers require technical support, plan and budget for this before making any agreements. The industry rule-of-thumb is that 20% of your resellers will generate 80% of your revenue. This means that you will spend time working with resellers that will not provide a return on your investment.

In reality some resellers will take on products to round off their product line to have a complete solution to present to their customers. A correctly executed market entry plan will convince resellers the product you are presenting is competitive in the market. Be prepared to provide advertising for your product, the resellers will not generate demand. The resellers' sales representatives will sell what they are most comfortable talking about as long as demand is there. You will need to manage your channels to ensure that your company and your products are represented in the best light. Proper training and incentives for the resellers' sales team will sell your product!

Structuring the deal using pay for performance is the only way to go. Do not take equity in a partnership without a performance component. Pay for performance also qualifies their level of commitment and interest. If you have revenue generating terms to the agreements you need to ensure that you maintain control of the accounts if the partnership should end. Do not make exclusive agreements unless you know that the channel will provide a financial guarantee. The complexity level of your product will determine which types of resellers to pursue. Diversification of channels will minimize the risk of failure.

Distributors

A distributor buys product at a discount from the manufacturer and then resells or licenses the products for a profit to their dealers or retailers. The size of the product discount offered to the distributor is in part based on the scope of the distributor's functions. Distributors typically have trained representatives and knowledgeable staff operating their offices and will have warehouse facilities to store and ship the product. Distributors usually take care of presale product demonstrations and will provide post sale service and support. If a distributor plans to spend substantial amounts of money marketing your products, they may require an exclusive territory and a long-term contract. U.S. law requires that they set their own prices after taking into consideration your wholesale price. Manufacturers can provide a suggested selling price but cannot dictate the price that the distributor offers their customers. This pricing cannot vary from distributor to distributor. Nevertheless, discounts based on volume can be offered.

Using distributors a manufacturer's out-of-pocket expense for entering the U.S. market will be low. The distributor usually bears the inventory and credit risk. The options available will differ because each distributor handles an array of different products. Depending upon the type of product, the demand, or service support requirements will determine whether you should use a distributor or your own sales representative. I am seeing a gradual shift to distributors handling more products on a consignment basis thereby reducing their risk and out-of-pocket expense.

Because distributors generally purchase product at a substantial discount you will receive a smaller percentage of each retail sales dollar than if you market your products through a sales representative. However, there are other costs to consider such as warehousing, order fulfillment, insurance, and taxes, that should influence your decision.

While traditional channel and distribution partnerships are well established in the U.S. there has been a rise in collaborating and alliance arrangements that are not distribution based. Reasons to partner include the traditional ones such as joint marketing and distribution as well as increased time-to-market, product development, customer retention, fulfillment, flexibility, and post sales support. Partnerships do not generally reduce expenses so it is important that there is some affect on revenue even if it is just to establish your credibility through an alliance with a well-recognized company. Managing a successful partnership is all about trust but at the same time you need to protect your intellectual property.

Systems integrators play a unique role and may constitute good partners for some companies but they tend to be service driven. There is little margin in hardware and software for them and they will typically require on the ground support from the supplier.

Sales Representation

A sales representative attains product knowledge in order to demonstrate and sell products to a customer. They become the face of the company to the customer. The sales representative depending upon their industry may stock inventory but does not takes title to the products and cannot bind a company to make the sale. The sales representative is usually limited to a specified geographic territory and can be either exclusive or nonexclusive to the manufacturers that they represent. By using a sales representative your out-of-pocket expenses of entering the U.S. market will be lower. Compensation can differ significantly based on geography and experience. Sales representatives can be paid on commission only or a percentage of sales. Others may work on a draw basis or are paid a salary plus bonus if they meet certain quotas.

Having a sales representative work on commission only can be a risky proposition to a foreign company because the representative could go months without being paid and may look to other sources of income to maintain their standard of living. Selling through a sales representative will net you a higher percentage of revenue than selling through distributors or licensees.

Using a sales representative may not be effective for mass-marketed computer software or for sophisticated technology products. Sophisticated products often require significant presale demonstration and customer education or post sale technical support. These services are not generally available from a sales representative. Sales representatives who handle multiple product lines also may not provide the focused attention needed for a new product introduction.

Companies will spend billions of dollars on personal selling to get their products to market. Sales representatives are usually your company's highest paid non-managers. Top salespeople usually work on a base salary and commission plus bonuses. Stay away from commission only sales because these sales representatives tend to go with other products in their portfolio that will bring them in quick and easy income. The real cost for the business is not the sales commissions paid it's the costs related to the difficulty in finding qualified customer prospects and the expense of long and complex sales cycles. With the advent of Web-based communities most of these members who are in more sophisticated markets are not interested in the typical sales "cold calling" methodology. They are looking to be cultivated and have a trust-based relationship with their vendor as well as the account executive or salesperson. The high-tech salesperson must be an expert in the technology being sold, have knowledge about the trends affecting their assigned customers, the ability to influence the market, and have the persuasion and the language communications skills required to influence their customers.

The local sales force is also your greatest source of information in that they are directly engaging with the customer and receive feedback as to customer requirements. It is essential that your sales process captures this feedback to use in future product development and re-finement. Hiring a suitable sales representative overseas is one of the most important decisions facing a non-U.S. exporter just starting in the region. Your local sales representative will be responsible for attracting channel sales partners and assisting them in growing sales for your products. An appropriate sales representative should have at least four to six years experience working in the local channel and have a broad background preferably in your company's specific product sector.

Additionally, because your sales representative will be your company's first point of contact for all sales and marketing efforts in the region, it is important that this person is well established in the industry and has a strong network of contacts. It is wise to spend your money on a highly skilled person who can hit the ground running. Remember, you get what you pay for.

Generally compensation would be part base salary and part commission. It is important to include metrics into the incentive scheme that drive the kind of behavior you would want to achieve. For example if you want excellent customer service and repeat business, reward your sales force for this and not just for new business.

When entering a new market initially there will be a certain ramp up period in which most likely there will be no or limited sales revenues, so most sales representatives during this period will require a guaranteed salary. Because of the estimated time for an initial sale will vary on the product being sold, having a commission only sale representative usually will not be in your best interest.

A sales team can be organized various ways in anticipation of future sales growth. Each of these methods will depend on your target customers and the overall goals of the company. The focus of these groups are:

- Territory arrangement where a representative is assigned a geographic area usually used for dispersed customers

- Product groups where detailed product knowledge or those with a wide product range are assigned to build up in-depth knowledge

- Customer groups where the sales force having complex customer requirements become knowledgeable about the industry and specific customers

Getting the size of your sales force right is essential as each new sales employee adds to your expenses but at the same time not hiring enough salespeople can impact on your revenues. This may mean that the smallest group of customers generates the largest revenue.

The scale and complexity of the market tends to defeat a newcomer without an experienced U.S. team to assist. What is required from foreign companies is that they have sufficient funds to last at least one year to manage their operations and to attract top caliber American executives and partners.

Very few foreign companies have the technology and unlimited funding to take on their U.S. competition. One possible solution is licensing elements of a company's core technology or intellectual property to a potential partner or perceived competitor. In some instances it is more advantageous to license your technology to a competitor than trying to compete with them.

Having a member of your executive or management team based in the target country does not always make sense. Sales and marketing as well as the day-to-day operations can be outsourced. At some point the Chief Technology Officer may need to have a base in the targeted country enabling him/her to meet and work with specific U.S. executives, especially those companies with sophisticated systems and software that would benefit from face-to-face meetings.

OEM and VARs

A license agreement will be required whenever you want to have a potential partner modify or manufacture the patented or copyrighted technology that has been developed. This applies to the use of confidential information along with them agreeing to distribute your product. An original equipment manufacturer (OEM) or value added reseller (VAR) is like a distributor, except that they must add value of some type, hardware or software, etc., when it resells or licenses your product. These arrangements can become quite intricate when the other party integrates your product into theirs. This can be accomplished through access to your application program interface or the source code to accomplish the integration of the two products. The agreement will usually have the OEM partner market the product under their name while a VAR generally markets the product under your company's name. When you grant the right to modify, manufacture, or duplicate your product, you negotiate to receive a royalty from the licensee rather than a price for the product sold.

Licensing arrangements provide greater flexibility in tailoring your product to the partner who better understands the needs of their customers and the overall market. It also provides a less costly way to establish your presence in the U.S. without opening offices or hiring additional staff. Customs, shipping, and fulfillment issues can be reduced by licensing technology rather than shipping final product, which becomes the responsibility of the partner. There may also be tax advantages for you in licensing the product because you would not have a permanent U.S. address.

The OEM or VAR will have greater access to how your technology works than do distributors or sales representatives. If your relationship with the OEM or VAR should fail it may leave you vulnerable because you would not only need a new channel to sell your product but your former partner will have intimate knowledge and access to your product. They could also become a possible competitor to you because they have a better grasp of the market and an existing customer base. Good legal consul is essential in developing OEM and VAR agreements.

Having a license agreement will net you an even smaller percentage of each retail sales dollar than if you market your products through a distributor. A U.S. licensee may be subject to withholding tax, depending on whether your country has entered into a taxation treaty with the U.S. This should be checked out with an international tax advisor prior to negotiations.

Subsidiary or Branch Office

A subsidiary has advantages over a branch office. Many companies export their goods directly to their own sales subsidiaries. The subsidiary then assumes the role of the independent distributor. By doing so the manufacturer:

- has control of selling operations in the foreign market;

- commits capital in a foreign country for the financing of accounts;

- limits liability to your investment;

- treats orders as if they originated from a U.S. company subject to U.S. taxes; and

- demonstrates to the customer a greater commitment to the U.S. market.

For many companies their first step is to set up a subsidiary. They do this to handle their manufacturing and to provide customer support. In this case they will continue to use the distribution channels that they established for product sales. As the company gains more experience in the market they tend to do more of their own localized marketing and sales.

U.S. Subsidiary

Deciding where to locate your business involves a number of marketing, legal, and financial factors. These include state property taxes, income taxes, incentives available for the specific type of business, and the skill level needed for your work force. Tax rates will vary considerably by location. Seven states do not levy any income tax. These are Texas, Washington, Alaska, Nevada, Wyoming, Florida, and South Dakota. Five states—Oregon, Delaware, Alaska, Montana, and New Hampshire have no sales tax. Most international companies will establish themselves in Delaware or California for business reasons.

U.S. subsidiaries initially tend to be sales and marketing or research and development operations rather than assembly or manufacturing operations. Incentives that are applicable to manufacturing operations such as reduced property taxes are not relevant to a sales and marketing operation.

In the United States a non-U.S. company may be subject to U.S. federal withholding tax on royalties received from technology licenses. In the U.S. a corporation is taxed as a separate legal entity. The business relationship between the foreign parent and U.S. subsidiary must be clearly defined and documented to keep the legal identities separate for both tax and liability purposes. The subsidiary should have a distributor, sales representative, licensee or other relationship with the parent, each reflected in a written agreement. Transactions between such related parties must reflect separation of the parties for IRS reporting purposes.

Most countries impose either a sales, value added tax or an income tax. A sales tax is a tax based on the sale price of a product while an income tax is based on income over an annual period made from such sales after deducting allowable expenses.

Branch Office

The branch office must qualify to do business with the state where it is located. The federal "branch profits tax" reduces the desirability of branch operations unless a tax treaty provides otherwise. Complex rules govern the "branch profits tax" and the allocation of expenses deductible from such income. Another important factor in favor of a subsidiary is that U.S. Internal Revenue Service (IRS) tax audits are limited primarily to the subsidiary and not the parent. For this reason most companies prefer to set up a U.S. subsidiary rather than a branch office.

Agencies

A market entry agency provides a foreign company a less expensive way to enter the market and can be an important part of a manufacturers' success. The agency may act as your manufacturer's representative but adds additional value by developing sales and distribution channels and handles daily operations for the foreign company. It can also manage the wholesale and retail accounts interested in your product by addressing any of their clients' questions and service concerns. There are many varieties of agencies each with a different focus or specialty. These can be strictly marketing, public relations, sales or different combinations of each business specialty. Unlike consultants, the market entry agency is focused on generating revenue for their clients and their success in the market. An agency's success can be measured by mutually established goals while a consultant normally bills by the hour and will provide the client with general advice. The benefits of using a market entry agency include:

- Increase in revenue from direct and/or indirect sales

- Reduced time-to-market

- Reduced risk

- Lower costs for market entry

- Elimination of the "learning curve" in language, cultural and business differences

- Faster response to partner and/or customer requests

- Having a knowledgeable agency can expedite the process providing you a competitive advantage

To realize success for their client an agency will develop successful partnerships, alliances and distribution channels that are well matched in terms of strategic fit and mutual benefit. Because they represent their client by becoming their client's face to prospective customers, it eliminates the uncertainties of dealing with a foreign company. An agency can leverage their client's position through their knowledge of the market and maneuver the business direction within that market. They do this by:

- analyzing the competitors' sales and distribution channels;

- defining and quantifying their client's value and benefits;

- providing lead generation and customer vetting; and

- managing the entire sales and marketing process.

The agency will develop customer specific presentations and a "product dashboard" for the select industry, sales channels, and customers. They should be prepared to provide specific product sales training to their distributor's network and sales representatives. They will broker the necessary agreements on your behalf with distributors, licensees, and customers. Their goal is to provide you with a direct presence while minimizing the risk and overcoming the barriers to entry.

Do not confuse sales or manufacturer's representatives with a market entry agency. A sales representative will demonstrate and explain the benefits of their products to the customer. The sales representative handles one or more manufacturers selling a complementary line of products. An agency usually will not have competing products or companies. An agency will have their own sales staff or consultants and will bring on experts in specific fields as required to assist their clients. The clients of market entry agencies could span almost every industry. Because of the complex nature of the products or technology being promoted, a market entry agency can take up to several months to establish the foundation for selling the product through the appropriate channels. A dedicated agency will present your products to a customer and negotiate the sale on your behalf. They will make a persuasive sales pitch to the customer and are able to answer technical and non-technical questions about the products and your company.

Both an agency and independent sales representatives may attend or participate in trade shows where new products and technologies are showcased. They also may attend conferences and conventions to meet clients.

Usually a company's sales representative will team with a technical expert to review the customer's account and explain the product in detail as well as answer questions to clarify the concerns of the customer. A sales representative makes the preliminary contact with customers, introduces the company's product and closes the sale. After a sale, the representative may make follow-up visits to ensure that the equipment is functioning properly and may even help train customers' employees to operate and maintain new equipment while an agency will ensure that this occurs. An agency selling consumer products will suggest how and where merchandise should be displayed. When working with retailers, they help arrange promotional programs and advertising.

Where both are focused on obtaining new accounts, an agency will monitor the sales, prices and products of your competitors. Both will spend much of their time traveling to and visiting with current clients and prospective buyers. They may show samples or catalogs that describe items their company stocks and inform customers about prices, availability, and ways in which their products can provide benefit. Sales representatives will handle numerous products from multiple manufacturers, which means your product could get lost in the shuffle unless it is a high profit easy to sell item. A sales representative may have different job titles. Manufacturers' agents or manufacturers' representatives, for example, are self-employed sales workers who own independent firms that contract their services to all types of manufacturing companies. Being dedicated to their clients an agency will provide the necessary time and attention to ensure their clients' success.

Getting Your Product through Customs

No matter what structure you decide on to bring your products to market you have to understand the customs intricacies of market entry. Before shipping product to the target country you will need to find out how the product will be classified and valued by customs and what procedures you must follow. In the United States all products must comply with U.S. Customs and the import procedures that they have established. Licensed customs brokers can assist you in this process. They can assist you in getting your products through customs by preparing the required entry forms. These forms describe the imported items, their custom's monetary value, the product's Harmonized Tariff Schedules and classification numbers.

The importer is required to classify products entering the U.S. market. The U.S. often imposes quotas and tariff sanctions on specific products and countries and may prohibit importation of products from certain embargoed countries. For medical devices, pharmaceuticals, and other products you may need to obtain product safety approvals from such agencies as the Food and Drug Administration or the Federal Communications Commission to name a few. By first checking out the customs procedures you save time and possible headaches later on. Customs duties and fees play a vital role in the final pricing of the product along with transportation, warehousing and fulfillment. In order to determine the customs duty owed, you will need to "value" the imported product using one of the specified five methods.

The one used most often by importers is the transaction value of the imported merchandise meaning the actual price paid or payable. The declared product value for entry purposes should be the same as the transfer price reported to the U.S. IRS. Imports from select developing countries may be eligible for duty-free entry into the U.S. under various preferential tariff programs. Examples of other preferential tariff programs include the North American Free Trade Agreement (NAFTA) and the U.S.-Israel Free Trade Agreement. Under these programs many tariffs are either reduced or eliminated.

Working with a European client trying to enter the U.S. market with their consumer products that were manufactured in China, I encountered a dilemma that a lot of importers will be faced with. For one set of their products the Harmonized Tariff Schedules (HTS) resulted in no additional fees added to the product. For the other set of products it became more difficult. The tariff listing varied from 15% to 45% depending on the materials used to manufacture the product and the products specific use. We had the export code, which did not match with the import tariff code. For the European company getting an accurate tariff code upfront would make the difference between making a profit or not. Trying to determine the correct HTS to be used turned out to be difficult even for experienced customs brokers. The customs broker eventually had to go directly to the government to get the tariff code resolved. By doing so the company was able to use the lower tariff code, which provided them the ability to sell their product in the United States.

U.S. law requires that all imported products be marked with the country of origin. When an imported product contains parts from different countries, the country of origin marking the product must reflect where the product underwent substantial transformation, which in most cases is the country where it was assembled. The Federal Trade Commission (FTC) also regulates the marking of products sold in the United States. U.S. assembled products that contain imported parts should be marked "Assembled in the USA." A product cannot be marked "Made in the USA" if the product contains any foreign parts or components.

Business Incubators

Incubators nurture young, mostly pre-market companies helping them to survive and grow during the early startup phase when they are most vulnerable. Incubators provide hands-on management assistance, coaching and where needed access to financing. They provide the introductions to critical business or technical support services. Incubators are especially suited to technical and service businesses. Incubators can take on many forms with some exclusively focused on biotechnology or alternative energy vehicles. Joining an incubator can help reduce your overhead by providing shared resources with other like-minded companies. The best incubators are those that also provide advice from experienced technology managers and introductions to a solid network of existing contacts.

7 Positioning for Global Advantage

The study of economic growth is too serious to be left to the economist.
E. J. Mishan

Opportunity is built on the principle that providing a product, service or an experience that can makes people's lives easier and more enjoyable will always be in demand. What I have found working with foreign start-up companies is that in many cases identifying a genuine consumer need and providing a solution for that need is missing. For many the need they are filling is localized to the market of their home country and has very little impact worldwide. I often hear from these entrepreneurs how their technology will revolutionize the world. These executives go on about the uniqueness of their technology but miss the key element, which is how their technology will provide customer value. Those companies who can answer how their product or technology will fulfill these needs with a clear and distinct benefit are in the best position to win market share. Meeting these requirements becomes the roadmap for business investment and success. I have interviewed many executives who casually assume that being in America guarantees success, not recognizing that perhaps it is their behavior that may be the strongest influence on failing to achieve the results they are seeking. Successful executives are of the belief that opportunity is attracted to new ideas with genuine concern for the needs of others. In other words, finding the customers "pain point" or those specific areas of concern that the customer needs help in solving. Certainly, some businesses such as those that specialize in novelty products (Pet Rocks) do nothing to minimize anyone's pain.

There is an array of alliance options available to those aggressive companies wanting to enter a new market. They range from intellectual property exchange to product integration, which can provide a solution for something that may be missing in the technology of either company. Alliances are made to advance common goals and to secure common interests. They are founded on the principles of exclusivity, mutual trust, the minimizing of risk, and the maximizing of reward. Vendors and suppliers base their relationship on the exchange of an asset that will eventually be sold. For foreign companies developing alliances may be an unfamiliar concept. Working together in a close-knit relationship with an unknown entity is not something the independent entrepreneur can just jump into even though it may be in their best interest. In many cases there are cultural barriers that can hinder the process. In many countries suppliers are generally free to decide to whom they will or will not sell a product. Yet, as we have seen in places like Saudi Arabia the ability to decide whose product you sell is not the norm. For many countries the right to sell and who you may work with may be limited. The U.S. is an open market where you cannot discriminate between whom you will sell a product nor can you boycott suppliers or competing resellers. If a supplier has a monopoly on the products being offered then the supplier may have an obligation to deal with all potential customers.

There are several methods for finding and qualifying value-added resellers (VARs), distributors, system integrators, and other types of partners. They can be found on the Internet or CDs can be purchased from research companies that create lists sorted by product type, services offered, and specialty focus. Leads should be qualified to those prospects best suited to your product or technology and the needs and requirements of your company. There are numerous conferences and publications as well as strategic partners who can be a good source of leads. If your product is complementary to an existing strong brand such as Oracle, Microsoft, SAP, IBM, or Google, you may be able to participate in their ongoing programs and events as well as using their Web sites to determine who their partners are and make an introduction.

Your VAR strategy should take into account regional population centers for determining the best geographic disbursement of your channel partners and their customer base. A single VAR may cover a broad rural or suburban territory, while multiple resellers will be required to support some of the more densely populated cities or regions. The end-user must always factor into your selection and the type of program you develop. If the government is a primary customer, you will need to determine VARs already have contracts in place with specific government agencies. You must also be prepared to manage their unique pricing, security, and documentation requirements. In recruiting a partner you will be required to remove much of the risk from them in the initial purchase and that may include providing no or low-cost evaluation units, free product training, and products on consignment.

Once you have them, you have to manage them. Reward programs, ongoing training, qualified lead referrals, joint calls to corporate cus- tomers, and other recurring revenue programs provide incentives to give you priority and maintain long-term loyalty. A Sales Promotion Incentive Fund (SPIF) is special money allocated to provide sales personnel with specific financial incentives geared towards supporting tactical or strategic company goals.

Alliances can go from an exchange of assets to a more complex strategic relationship based upon the intellectual property integrated into the relationship. The degree of trust, control, risk, and reward are the basis of determining the type of relationship and the time associated with building the foundation for future growth.

I have found that it is easier to terminate distributor agreements in the U.S. than in Europe or Latin America. A supplier in the U.S. is usually most at risk when it terminates an existing distributor agreement. I have witnessed a terminated reseller claiming such termination was part of an effort to enforce an unlawful agreement regarding price-fixing or other types of restraint. To reduce this possibility it is best to avoid extensive restrictions on the way the reseller does business and the payment of fees other than for products. Suppliers can only provide a suggested retail price but cannot set the retail price for a product unless they are selling it themselves. If a high degree of control is deemed necessary over resale practices you may want to establish a wholly owned subsidiary to handle U.S. sales.

Range of Alliance Options

1. General suppliers carry similar products from different manufacturers alongside others in their catalog that may or may not compete with your products. These suppliers focus on products that usually provide them with the greatest return on investment. Many have their own Web sites and sales representatives for product sales. Each has their own specific requirements from their suppliers. Many will buy and import the product from the manufacturer. Most will focus on specific product categories and have an established customer base. To get noticed it is advisable to have a exceptional product that can compliment other products already being listed in the catalog. Product information provided must be clear and concise and images should be included. General supplier agreements are the simplest form of vendor relations.

2. OEM suppliers purchase products or components from manufacturers and retail them under their company's name. Most leading companies such as Cisco Systems or General Motors are OEM suppliers of other company's products. By being an OEM supplier you will have to drive down the cost of production as well as administrative overhead so that you can provide the purchasing company the lowest possible price for the product. The advantage for the purchasing company is that they can obtain the needed components or products without owning and operating any manufacturing facilities. They are also in a better position to switch out components or products, as demand requires.

3. Collaborative relationships are based on agreements between companies working together to leverage the others' IP instead of developing their own. This formula can be used for the co-production of products especially in different countries where the development base would be too expensive. Collaborative

relationships could include co-promotion, cross licensing, and teaming together for joint bidding on projects and joint research and development. Collaborative relationships provide an underutilized means for foreign companies wishing to expand into new markets. It is difficult to view the U.S. market from overseas because foreign companies do not have firsthand knowledge of products, technologies or competitor companies. Having a defined collaborative relationship enhances the resources needed to gain market share.

4. Customer alliances can take different forms. One example would be when a customer purchases a specific product but also may invest in the company expecting future returns as the product is adapted by the customer's industry. Another example would be when a specific product could have a major influence on an entire industry and may provide the first mover advantage over their competitors. This arrangement provides for more exclusivity and the development of specialty products, service and support, and co-location of personnel to modify the program to the customers' needs. If funding is required to help finish the technology and bring the product quicker to market it may be easier to seek funding from a potential customer rather than the venture community.

5. A sourcing partnership is an alliance agreement among several exclusive companies in the supply chain process that come together to manufacture one complete product. This partnership is designed to find the best product companies while improving the purchasing activities for the companies involved by following a defined process for cost control and efficiency. The partnership helps to provide a new supply structure along with tracking the movement of product located anywhere in the world. These sourcing partnerships can be found in the automobile and aerospace industries as well as others. Working with a group of partners from around the world does have drawbacks such as products being delayed or not fitting specifications such as in the case of Boeing's new 787 Dreamliner. In other cases like the Japanese "Kieretsu," once established can be very effective in bringing product to market.

6. Strategic integration alliances provide for the incorporation of one company's intellectual property and systems with that of a partner's system. This type of alliance is commonly used in high technology where tech companies will have developer programs

to support the integration of one company's IP into another. Principal names such Apple, Microsoft, and Yahoo will use these partnerships to round off their product offerings and to expand their feature sets. Doing an integration alliance requires resources by both parties. It may require joint technology development and possible value chain re-engineering to ensure that the process is successful. Exploiting this type of partnership requires the ability to perceive the potential then to articulate it to the other party. Doing this type of alliance minimizes the need for establishing a U.S. sales presence but in most cases may require local engineering and support staff depending on where product development is occurring.

7. Equity joint ventures are business relationships entered into by two or more companies to share the expense and profits of a particular business project. These projects can take on a variety of scope such as pure research and development, joint product production, shared distribution, sales, and marketing programs. Emerging companies have been able to use this business strategy to good advantage over the years as investor companies provide the equity for these companies to get started and later to become a spin in to the investor company or set-up for an initial public offering. Both parties should know up-front what they wish to derive from the partnership and what the exit strategy would be in the future. The leading cause for failure of joint ventures is that there may be a hidden agenda by either party or there may not be a true desire to uphold the agreement. In the competitive nature of Silicon Valley one company may invest in other just to kill off any other potential suitor from buying the targeted company. In the long run this tactic may be cheaper than letting the targeted company enter the market and compete head-on with the buyer's technology. Other factors that can have a devastating impact on joint ventures include changes in the market place, technology that is late to market as well as regulatory uncertainties. Among the most significant benefits derived from joint ventures are saving money and reducing risk through capital and resource sharing. Joint ventures also give smaller companies the chance to work with larger ones to develop, manufacture, and market new products. They also give companies of all sizes the opportunity to increase sales, gain access to wider markets, and enhance technological capabilities.

8. Spin out, spin in. A spin out is when a company segregates sections of itself into a separate business entity. The "spin out" company takes assets, intellectual property, technology, and existing products from the parent organization giving it potential to grow existing ideas that had been languishing. In most cases the management teams are from the same parent company. The parent company or organization offers support doing one or more of the following:

- By investing equity in the new firm

- Being the first customer of the spin out

- Providing incubation space

- Providing services such as legal, finance, technology support, etc.

A spin in is where employees break off from the parent company for about two years to run their own venture and then rejoin the parent firm. A classic spin in I worked on at Cisco Systems was the spin out and then spin in of Andiamo Systems, a Fibre Channel switch maker. Andiamo was created by several senior Cisco executives who were threatening to leave Cisco to pursue other opportunities. To keep them, it was believed that Cisco promised they would receive special compensation for their efforts. Andiamo came to life in January of 2001 and just four months later Cisco gave the company an $84 million investment. Following that investment, Cisco received a 44% stake in the start-up and the right to acquire the company. Andiamo used Cisco facilities and had Cisco staff supporting the development and operations of the spin out. Even though Andiamo was supposed to be a separate company, the process was designed from the beginning to be spun back into Cisco later. In August of 2002, Cisco decided to go ahead and acquire Andiamo. Hardware start-ups typically sell for much less than software start-ups due to the different natures of the businesses. Hardware usually has lower margins, more costs and tends to become standardized more quickly.

9. Merger and acquisition (M&A) is a corporate strategy dealing with buying, selling and the combining of different companies that can aid company growth rapidly without having to create another business entity. An acquisition, also known as a takeover or a buyout, is the buying of one company by another. An acquisition

may be friendly or hostile. In the former case, the companies co-operate in negotiations; in the latter case, the takeover target is unwilling to be bought or the target's board has no prior knowl-edge of the offer. There are multiple types of mergers dealing with how each company relates to their customers and the market. In practice, however, actual mergers of equals do not happen very often. Usually one company will buy another and as part of the deal's terms, allowing the acquired firm to proclaim the action is a merger, even if it is technically an acquisition.

While traditional channel and distribution partnerships are a well estab-lished business concept, there has been a rise in strategic partnering and alliance arrangements that are not distribution based. Improved communications and globalization are often attributed as two of the forces behind this rise. Reasons to partner include the traditional joint marketing and distribution as well as increased time-to-market, product development, customer retention, fulfillment, flexibility, and post sales support.

Whenever you are considering taking on a new partner it is essential that you look at your business objectives and consider what value the new partner brings to the plan. Unless there is some definitive benefit to you, you need to consider seriously if this is the right partner for you. Partnering for the sake of it can be an enormous drain on your resourc-es. You need to establish partnership agreements that mitigate risk while increasing mutual benefit. Partnerships do not generally reduce expenses so it is important that there is some affect on revenue even if it only enhances your reputation. Running a successful partnership is all about trust but at the same time you need to protect your intellectual property.

Marketing and Sales

The insight of Robert Louis Stevenson that "everyone lives by selling something" applies even more today than in his time. Market success will be based on the ability to sell yourself, your product or both. In the United States the consumer will buy based on the experience being provided, the brand and how the product is being positioned.

Presentation matters because there are few best products or services. Value is only based on perception and how it is managed and created makes all the difference.

To be successful in selling products to the U.S. market you need to understand how to sell for repeatable and profitable results. People buy because of:

- Confidence in you

- Your company's integrity

- The service you provide

- An effective delivery system

- The belief that in selecting your product they have made the right decision

The way to become profitable is choosing and closing the sale with those customers who can potentially provide revenue over a long period. A sustainable value and a solid reputation will do more to enhance your profitability than your pricing.

Not all customers are the same. Your dilemma is how to balance the cost of acquiring a new customer against the time involved maintaining your existing customers. Getting to know first how your prospective customer perceives your product's value will determine which customers to concentrate your efforts on. Articulate the value for people to understand what you offer. In many cases you will find that confidence equals value.

More money is spent on direct sales than all other forms of marketing combined. The average cost of closing a sale in the U.S. can range from $300 to $600 or more with an average of five calls for each sale to close the deal. This varies greatly depending on the complexity of the product and the market.

Don't Change That Channel!

Most companies sell their products and services three ways:

- Directly—by their own sales force or company owned outlets

- Indirectly—through what is termed "the channel," which includes dealers, distributors, retailers, resellers, and systems integrators

- Web-based—through the use of Web sites and Web stores

In a channel agreement the channel will pay the supplier for their product(s) and then sell the product to their customer base. In the United States channels exist in almost every industry where they have been vital to increasing product sales for manufacturers. They provide product awareness, customer service and support and in many cases technology solutions for their customers. Foreign manufacturers can generate 40% to 60% of their sales with this type of business partnership. Making the product irresistible to the channel through product positioning becomes critical because in reality you are selling either

1. a need, which will solve a problem, or
2. a want, which fulfills a desire.

With a large percentage of sales coming directly from the channel, successfully managing and working with them is clearly one of the most important marketing and sales strategies a manufacturer can endeavor to do. The rise of the Internet has made the buyer much more powerful than the vendor. For technology companies, experts predict that the channel will account for up to 65% of all product technology sales to small and medium sized businesses. With this kind of growth, the channel is a key driver for market leading companies. The challenge for a foreign company is the ability to manufacture and ship the product to the channel while meeting the time-to-market, service and quality standards of mature markets.

Sales and Marketing Options

Alliances are based on value creation through product or service integration needed by both companies. Most foreign companies first tend to establish a direct sales force to penetrate a new market rather than an alliance. This way they believe that they can have better control of their sales while maintaining the integrity of their marketing message. When this approach doesn't work or becomes too costly they will re-evaluate their overall distribution strategy. There are several sales and marketing options to choose from:

1. Multi-brand retailers will carry multiple brand named products from a selection of suppliers. Many retailers will concentrate on specific categories of products such as electronics, furniture or plumbing supplies. Depending upon the industry, these retailers can also manufacture products under their own label, re-brand their private label to other companies and most likely will out-source manufacturing of their store-brand items to multiple third parties on a cost and quality basis. Often you will find that the same manufacturers that produce brand-labeled goods produce store-brand products for different retailers. This is usually done in the food and beverage industry but the concept can apply to any industry. Store-brand products are generally less expensive than their national-brand counterparts because the retailer can optimize production and forgo any advertising and marketing.

2. Exclusive dealers provide exclusivity to the manufacturer's product(s) and will not carry competing products from other suppliers. An exclusive automobile dealer carries only Mercedes Benz and no other make. Hallmark Cards, Tumi Luggage, and Victoria Secret stores will only carry their own merchandise or merchandise made only exclusively for them. Providing products for exclusive use by a retailer may limit your expansion capabilities but depending on the dealer can propel your company into the market. An alternative is an exclusive license that provides for the intellectual property or the brand to a company for their use.

3. Incremental sales channels are independent channels that usually have knowledge of the product category and sell the product on an as needed basis to increase their revenues. This channel is unconnected to your direct sales channel but can bring

in additional sales. These may be independent sales representatives who will sell your product line as an adjunct to the standard lines that they are carrying.

4. Co-product promoter is a marketing arrangement where one company works with you to advertise your products along with theirs in a promotion or a sponsorship arrangement. Both companies will share the cost of marketing. You see this done at concerts and sporting events where multiple companies are promoted. McDonalds has been doing this for years by tying their Happy Meals with popular movie characters.

5. Value added resellers generally market product under the manufacturer's name. When you grant the right to modify, manufacture or duplicate your product, you negotiate to receive a royalty from the licensee rather than a price for the product sold. The VAR will usually handle the engineering and integration to bring the product lines together. A VAR will have a sales force, a service and support function as well as the ability to provide training to the customer.

6. Systems integrators are companies that will help their customers to bring together product components from multiple manufacturers into one working system. They accomplish this using their own staff and co-locating their personnel at the client's site and by re-engineering existing processes to ensure operations with the new integrated products. System Integrators used to be an important part of the sales process because their recommendations were viewed as impartial. For most small foreign suppliers the SI will do little unless there is a joint sales cycle and immediate money to be made for both parties. An offshoot of the systems integrator are multiple partner solution providers that will integrated multiple products and other technology and provide a unified marketing approach and delivery of the combined solution.

7. Marketing joint venture is similar to the alliance joint venture where two or more parties undertake marketing activities together. The participating companies will develop a unified business strategy to go-to-market together. Usually there is no equity stake involved. The purpose is to leverage the economies of scale as well as to reduce the costs and risks of developing your own marketing campaigns. You see this strategy used in sporting events such as the Olympic Games with its numerous sponsors.

8. Acquired sales channels are created when a company goes out specifically searching for established sales and distribution companies for building their own sales team. Getting quality salespeople is the partial goal along with acquiring existing customer accounts. The key to the deal is the experience of the channel's sales team in selling complimentary products to yours. If your distribution partner is selling other suppliers' products there may be potential conflicts that have to be handled prior to any deal being closed.

9. Direct sales are those accomplished face-to-face usually done at the customer's location by an independent or an employee sales representative. Because the salesperson is the first point of contact, it is important that this person is well established in the industry and has a strong network of contacts. If the sales representative is also a member of the online community he is trying to influence, this becomes another form of direct sales. This individual should know how to get to the community influencers to reinforce the vendor's message.

There is only one way for a foreign company to achieve growth in a market and that is to increase its customer base. This is accomplished by reaching new customers in existing markets or by entering new markets. It is my experience that most customers want products that provide uncomplicated, reliable functionality rather than unnecessary embellishments. When you look at the way customers use computer software they tend to use a fraction of the functions that are available to them.

Before selecting the channel determine if the alliance will be profitable, too risky or if it has a limited return for the amount of time expended. If it is too risky or limits your time, it should not be sought.

Resellers are as varied as the products they carry. Some are generalized, selling many products from different manufacturers, while others are more specialized servicing specific product lines or particular vertical industries such as banking or retail. There are many misconceptions about what the distribution channel does and does not do to help their manufacturers. The realities of the resellers are:

• Resellers need to be convinced that the product is competitive.

- Leads provided to your resellers will not always be followed up.

- Resellers do not generate demand. Demand generation is up to you.

- Resellers will take on a product to round off their catalog.

- Resellers will sell what they are most comfortable talking about and as long as it makes them money.

- Resellers won't always read your marketing materials.

Managing the Channel

In today's competitive environment it has become increasingly harder to find channel partners that will carry your product. Unless you have a unique product offering, most potential channel partners have already combined products and services from different suppliers to construct their product sales plan. It is not uncommon that 80% to 90% of a reseller's revenue comes from only two or three companies that they represent. The problem that foreign companies are up against is the indifference of the reseller. In order to get the resellers interest, try focusing on the products that will bring reseller's revenue. To get representation make sure your products blend in or compliment the others in their catalog. Even though revenue is a consideration, the reseller's are predisposed to view the product from a risk anticipating that the product may not sell and they would be left with unwanted inventory. There is also the possibility that with increased sales you will eventually set up your own direct sales efforts and drop them. Finally they are unsure of foreign companies because they do not know if you have the staying power to bring the product to market.

To be effective with the reseller you may want to use your social network and have them communicate with the reseller's sales team to influence them about the value of your products. Salespeople are usually open to new products because they receive part of their income from commissions. They are also closer to the customer and if there is perceived demand they likely will tell their management.

How Best to Recruit Resellers

The best ways to recruit resellers is by doing your research and being prepared to address the following:

1. Explain the value of your product(s) for their customers.
2. Establish definitive pricing policies.
3. Demonstrate a process for fulfilling orders.
4. Have a comprehensive service and support plan.
5. Provide localization if required to meet the need of the market segment.
6. Make available marketing materials including brochures and product sheets.
7. Provide product training if required.
8. Proactively create market demand and let the reseller know your plans.

Once the initial contact with the channel is made I would recommend sending them a sample of your product along with a product sheet so they can conduct their own evaluation. Providing them information on your company's go-to-market strategy, product pricing and support capabilities would also be helpful for their decision making. The more you can assist them the better off you will be. Be proactive in providing a Memorandum of Understanding (MOU) to determine the basics of the relationship. Give them a ninety day decision window to determine if there is a market for your products and follow-up if you haven't heard from them. Be careful of distributors who may approach you with a potential customer. You might make the one sale, but if you sign an agreement and they make no further sales, you may actually lose better opportunities by being tied to that one reseller. Like an acquisition, a reseller may also take on your product solely to keep you out of the market. This is rare, but it has occurred. The challenge though is finding a reseller that will actually sell your products on a regular basis.

Selling the Way Customers Want to Buy

As the technology market becomes more intricate, customers have been looking toward their suppliers for a total integrated solution rather than a set of component products. This demand has forced suppliers to form ecosystems of vendors that involve many different types of channel and alliance relationships. Because of the nature of these relationships the partners' role has shifted where companies may find themselves competing with their partners. In this case, you risk loss of direct interaction with the customer, possibly resulting in reduced product margins and support information.

Few resources exist either through government sponsored programs or country supported chambers of commerce to provide companies with the insights and tools required to develop a competitive market advantage. The result has been that many manufacturing companies take what little government support is offered, which only results in fulfilling the government's agenda. Nevertheless, these companies once they have been here will eventually pursue private support to accomplish their market entry objectives. Representatives of these government programs treat the channel as an afterthought only because they are unfamiliar with it. Only after the foreign company discovers the high cost of direct sales do they seek the use of agencies or channels to increase their revenues. To manage the channel effectively requires time and dedication. Foreign companies lack the persistence required to manage effectively through and with their channel. Consider that companies such as IBM, Cisco Systems, AT&T, and others collectively have more than 50,000 channel partners, which requires effective management of their accounts.

The challenge for the manufacturer is to build a strong marketing strategy to sell the way customers want to buy. As simple as this sounds the unpredictability of your customers makes this the most challenging task that few companies are prepared to handle alone. Even manufacturers that have established channel programs find it difficult working with the channels to sustain a dependable partnering experience. The scale of the U.S. is so large that a simple increase or decrease in sales can mean hundreds of millions of dollars. The ability for your company and its brand to connect with customers in innovative and distinctive ways will make it unsurpassed in the market like Apple Computer and Pixar Entertainment.

Consumers alter their purchasing behavior based on a changing flow of information, evolving technology and increasing price pressures. The channel may lose market share if it doesn't keep pace by facilitating the procurement of goods and services to maintain their existing customers and to acquire new ones. Because the introduction of the Internet and the growth of social media the world has greatly changed in the way business is being conducted. As author Nicholas Johnson observed, "It used to be that people needed products to survive. Now products need people to survive." To get those new and innovative products to the buyer is difficult to do on your own. To get to your customer today you have to rely on the marketing power of the media and Internet.

Finding Channel Partners

There is a broad range of resellers available in the U.S. Some resellers will only sell general pre-packaged software and hardware products, while others are more specialized servicing particular vertical industries. The complexity level of your product will determine which types of resellers to pursue. The first step in setting up a channel program is to carefully look at your company's objectives and plan a program that is geared towards meeting those objectives.

Companies should have a reseller kit ready before approaching any potential channel partner. This kit should contain the following:

- Program Description

- Program Benefits including:

  - Training

  - Local representation

  - Access to an existing customer base

  - Demonstration products

  - Technical support

- Marketing Materials that have been professionally produced

- A program that contains specific quarterly buy-in and sell-through requirements

- Reseller/Dealer Agreements drafted by a U.S. lawyer that outline the following:

  - Agreement terms

  - The rights of the dealer

  - Dealer obligations

  - License to use your logos and trademarks

  - Ownership of property rights

  - Non-disclosure of information

  - Warranties

  - Termination of the agreement

The United States offers foreign companies easy access to the largest and most dynamic market if the right method of distribution is selected and the legal procedures are followed. It is good to develop and maintain a wide range of channel partners with a broad base of customers. Utilize what you excel in and outsource any unfamiliar operating functions. You may want to combine several of these approaches because they are not mutually exclusive. For example, a license agreement may allow the licensee to purchase final product from you for resale. They may also want to manufacture and distribute your product. Finally they may want to create a joint venture to develop and market new products together.

Building the Partnerships

Building successful partnerships will require work on the part of both parties. The foundation of the arrangement is that both parties have something to gain otherwise the partnership will not last. The tendency that I have seen is that if the partnership doesn't produce tangible results early on, interest will wane and the partnership will dissolve. To establish a solid structure for support and cooperation these issues should be addressed:

1. **Define the partnership objectives** - Partnerships are established for a variety of reasons. They can be for leads and revenue generation. The purpose should be clearly defined as well as the exit strategy if the agreement doesn't work out.

2. **Select partners** - Identify and select partners capable of supporting your specific company's objectives. Often the most appropriate partners for your needs may have other arrangements and are not available.

3. **Due diligence** - Research their experience and focus on whether or not they can meet your objectives.

4. **Structure the deal** - The structure, to be successful needs a performance aspect that qualifies the level of commitment and interest. If you have revenue generating components to the agreement you need to maintain control of the accounts if the partnership should end.

Managing the Partnership

Once you have a contract the work is just beginning. The execution and management of the agreement for a reseller to sell your products is a full time job. Because your products are yours and not your resellers', your reseller will never be as enthusiastic as you are about selling your products. Work with your partner to set up sales and marketing programs. Conduct quarterly and annual reviews. Take into consideration local market conditions and trends, what has been happening in their business, etc. If they've missed sales goals, you need to know why. The more you can assist the reseller, the better off your company will be.

There are other considerations when marketing high technology products by way of distributors. Not maintaining a physical product may have its advantages or price competition may make some distribution agreements less attractive. The wholesale price to a distributor may be higher than the typical royalty paid by a licensee for the right to reproduce and package the product. To be competitive with third party products you may need to license technology rather than sell product through distribution.

But You Gotta Know the Territory!

Your sales and business development staff should be the greatest source of information regarding the desires of the specific customers with whom you wish to do business. It is essential that you have the processes in place to capture this feedback to use in positioning the product for the prospective customer and for future product development and refinement.

Companies wishing to pay only on commission will find themselves at a disadvantage because in general those that would accept this type of payment arrangement usually are your junior salespeople. For a company wishing to enter the market, your best return would be either to hire an agency or find a seasoned sales representative for the customers you are targeting.

If you are considering hiring a direct sales representative then I would recommend that that person be local given that culture affects sales style and purchasing behaviors. Local hires also have valuable established connections and networks. More money is spent on direct sales than all other forms of advertising combined. Your local sales representative will be responsible for:

- Attracting channel sales partners

- Assisting them in growing sales of your products

- Participating in trade shows

- Working with advertising and public relations firms

- Assisting in your overseas marketing efforts

A competent sales representative should have at least four to six years' experience working with the channels and have a broad background preferably in your company's specific product segment.

A sales representative for an overseas office should also have experience working in both sales and marketing. This is important because, as your company first enters the market your sales representative will most likely handle these multiple responsibilities.

Structuring the Sales Force

There are several ways to organize your sales force depending on your product and customer base. A territory arrangement works best when there are geographically dispersed customers and a sales representative is assigned to a specific area. The customer sales potential is the best indication of territory performance.

When there are technical products requiring in-depth product knowledge a product group arrangement may work best because the sales representative requires product understanding needed during the sales process.

Enterprise companies with complex business requirements often focus their sales force around customers in identifiable vertical industries. For example one sales team may focus exclusively on banking while another group will focus on the automotive industry. This allows the sales force to become very knowledgeable about the industry.

Systems integrators play a very strong role and may constitute good partners for some companies but they tend to be service driven as there is little margin in hardware and software for them so they will typically require product support from the supplier.

The number one mistake is simply trying to do too much with too little capital. You need modest expectations that are in line with the limited budget that typical non-U.S. companies have relative to their U.S. counterparts. Another mistake is not hiring enough American help soon enough. On the surface the market here often feels like a bigger version of your home country and it is easy to get over confident from positive feedback you receive. Unfortunately, the reality is not much useful business comes from this feedback. It's just that Americans tend to be more agreeable than most. It is almost impossible as a newcomer to get to the decision makers quickly. The complexity of U.S. business often impedes navigating a company's hierarchy without experienced U.S. support on your side.

In other countries you can attend industry events and meet the central players whereas in the United States you can attend the same type of events and not meet any of them. Prepare to be referred elsewhere by the group you would like to recruit because they may have all the clients that they can currently manage. On the other hand, if they are too easy to engage be wary because they may lack experience and trained personnel.

Contracts between Parties

Contract terms can be as varied as the number of partners and customers. Most alliance and sales contracts between parties have a standardized format. Being new to the market you will find that most partners and distributors have developed templates for standardizing their contracts. If your country is a member of the Convention on Contracts for the International Sale of Goods (CISG), you should consider applying this convention to your agreements with the U.S. company. CISG is an international treaty that automatically applies whenever a contract for the sale of goods is entered into between member companies whose governments have ratified the treaty. In some cases the companies may decide not to include this in their contract, which is true for many U.S. channels as recommended by their legal counsel. This is because CISG has no statute of fraud and acceptance of a verbal offer will be binding even if there is no written contract confirming the agreement.

In the U.S. the sale of products from your U.S. subsidiary to distributors or customers is governed by the Uniform Commercial Code (UCC). U.S. business agreements are usually more specific than either Asian or European agreements. In a binding agreement under the UCC the parties must include:

- Product pricing

- Quantity to be ordered

- Type of goods to be sold

- Distributor's obligations

- Intellectual property provisions that apply to:

  - Reverse engineering

  - Use restrictions

  - Confidentiality of information provided

- Governing jurisdiction

- Dispute resolution procedures

Agreement terms may be implied by the parties' common trade practices.

Warranties

There are two types of product warranties that companies provide their customers, implied and express:

1. Implied warranties exist without a written agreement and stipulate:

   - Products must be of average quality

   - Products may not infringe on a third party's intellectual property rights

   - Products must be suitable for the purposes for which they are sold

2. Express warranties are the seller's guarantee as regards:

   - Quality of material

   - Workmanship

   - Performance to written specifications

   - Freedom from defects

The duration of a warranty is usually limited to a specific time period following the purchase of a product. The warranty also covers the options available in case of a product defect. Due to the potential for a lawsuit, I would suggest seeking out legal advice prior to marketing your product in order to limit your liability.

8 The New Silk Road

The secret of success is constancy to purpose.
Benjamin Disraeli

The Internet, social media, and other technologies are drastically changing the international business environment; often in ways most companies are not yet aware. The unlimited access to information and increasing global competition from emerging countries have tended to commoditize entire industries and forced them to relocate their manufacturing offshore. Companies are experiencing downward pressures on their product prices and margins like never before. They are being asked to trade their products on a consignment basis thereby assuming more risk and financial burden. When faced with these changing demands from customers to lower prices and assume more risk, the value-added approach to product marketing will no longer work. Companies will search for market niches worldwide to try to overcome the risk and commodity pressure thus trying to maintain their margins and differentiate them from the competition.

Some of today's international business dealings are reminiscent of the pre-Internet economy. In the new economy sharing the risk, product consignment, and the process of commoditization is inevitable. In a world where customers have access to many vendors through alternative means both online and off, the only way to make money is by continually trying different business models while lowering your cost structure so that you can compete on price. While the Europeans are adapting to these changes we are still seeing hesitancy by the Chinese and South Koreans to develop new business models. I encourage companies to develop a well thought-out strategy rather than a knee-jerk response to competitive pressures and changing conditions in the U.S. marketplace.

Commoditization and Product Pricing

Developing a pricing strategy for a foreign market involves knowledge of five key factors:

1. The competition you are facing
2. The customers perception of your company
3. The financial soundness of your company
4. The perceived value of the product
5. Your marketing objectives

In understanding each of these elements you can establish a product price range according to the market and your targeted customer. By looking at product pricing long-term you can establish internal price targets, which can be modified as market conditions change. Pricing is primarily a function of managing margins and costs. By continually reviewing your pricing structure you can change your margins or eliminate costs to be more competitive. The goal is to find new ways to keep your pricing competitive and fair. Because margins are key when dealing with a discount mentality you may want to select your newest unfamiliar products and promote them at a limited discount.

When I go to the Napa Valley and other wine tasting regions of California I expect a day of new experiences. I always seek out unexplored wineries and enjoy sampling new and different wines, but I am disappointed when the wine maker offers their mediocre wines for tasting. By treating everyone like neophytes they are putting off those more seasoned wine buyers who are more discriminating in their tastes. Their selling and pricing strategy is to first hook the novice customer on the less expensive wine hoping to eventually have them move up to the premium, more expensive ones.

There are more than 2,800 wineries in California with more than 100 different grape varietals being produced. California is the fourth-leading wine producer in the world, after Italy, France, and Spain. Although it produces most of the wine made in the United States, California wines face more competition these days from distinctive wineries located in New Zealand, Chile, Australia as well as Europe. So what happens when a larger competitor decides to enter a niche market? Most small wineries know that they cannot compete on price. The large wineries can sell their wines for less than it costs the small ones to make and bottle. To stay competitive most will follow a two-stage strategy:

1. Review their customers to determine which niches and distribution channels are most secure.
2. Focus all of their resources on dominating those areas.

On one excursion to the Napa Valley I was looking for wineries that I hadn't experienced before. Arriving at a newly purchased winery that dated back over one hundred years my impression of the refurbished grounds and building lead me to believe I was in for an amazing experience. The owner was truly an oenophile, having a reputation for appreciating fine Italian wines and I assumed he would be serving his quality wines. Unfortunately like so many of his competitors the varietals that I was being charged to taste were standard, unimpressive fare. I inquired if they released any premium wines. They said yes, but they weren't pouring those today. After tasting the sampling being offered I went on my way writing this winery off as mediocre. A month later a friend invited me to dinner and mentioned he was serving a special reserve wine from a new winery that he recently discovered. He was so impressed he joined their wine club and was anxious for me to taste his new find. I was equally anxious knowing his palette for fine wines. So when he presented the bottle, I was wary because I recognized the label. I told him I had visited this winery and had not tasted anything to my liking. I sampled his selection and it was excellent. I inquired if he was able to taste before he joined their club. The answer was simple; he was introduced to the wine maker by a friend. It was a shame that I as well as the general public did not have the same experience because we did not know the wine maker nor were we in his network. The company lost my business because they failed to accommodate my request or even advertise their premium wines.

Then there are wineries such as Falcor Wine Cellars, which took a different approach to establishing themselves. I first became aware of this winery when the owner provided free samples of his award winning premium chardonnay in the bar area of Brannan's Grill in Calistoga, California. The premium chardonnay he was pouring was over 90 points according to *Wine Spectator* magazine. The wine was excellent and having decided to have lunch at this restaurant I ordered a full bottle of this luscious, buttery, olive oil in a glass, Chardonnay. To my surprise the winery owner came over to pour the wine and explain his philosophy of wine making. It was a wonderful experience. Falcor Wines have been consistent in quality and value and are appreciated by those of discerning taste. Falcor used the reverse approach by providing the customer with the best they had to offer even though it was in limited supply, unlike other wineries whose premium wines are unavailable for tasting. If only the other wineries would take this approach they too might have created a memorable experience and lifelong customer.

Customers, no matter what country they are from, will always appreciate a memorable buying experience. In the case of wine they would likely move up to the more expensive varietals if they were treated differently from the start. It is all in the marketing strategy, presentation, and salesmanship of the owner and staff. Wine is a good example of how pricing can affect product sales but also how marketing and sales can influence the purchase of the product and overall customer loyalty.

Advertising, merchandising, and product promotion can play a vital role in influencing the way a customer chooses a product. It is hard to determine how the entire shopping experience affects the purchasing decisions of the customer. Today's sophisticated consumer is influenced by many different criteria in selecting a brand or a company. The age of the decision maker and peer influence play an ever greater role in this process. Retailers have changed their buying and merchandising decisions to cater to younger buyers.

In business, the younger executives look at different criteria than their older counterparts in making their decisions. They want to be sold to differently and will use the Internet first to get information prior to having a conversation with the supplier to find out about the company and its products. But everyone enjoys being catered to and there is no better way to experience this than taking a trip to a supplier's customer briefing center on their Gulfstream to learn about their newest products. Then the perks follow such as tickets to the Super Bowl or reserved seating for the Rose Parade just to thank them for their business but ultimately it depends on your product, price and service to retain these key customers.

I was curious how customers purchase products such as wine from hundreds of different varietals and brands on the shelf. To find out I went to a local wine merchant with a graphic designer friend of mine, Larry Hausen of RuffHaus Design Studio. Through his use of eye catching designs he was able to increase ticket sales and brand awareness for the Golden State Warriors. By his exceptional capability of knowing what images will influence the consumer to buy, he was able to pick nine out of the ten best selling red wines being sold just by looking at the label on the bottle. This was independent of the price or brand name. Larry's philosophy is that customers need to feel something for the product before they will buy it. Customers are initially drawn to the label or packaging. His choices were confirmed by the store manager. This was the first of the five criteria consumers use in purchasing a product. The others are:

- They are familiar with the brand

- They have tried or used the product before

- The product was recommended by a person they trust

- The product's price

In reviewing the criteria it becomes apparent that if you take these factors together and add a positive customer experience it explains the impact of social media and how it is influencing the way products are bought and sold.

In the competitive world of wine sales, name brand wineries will reward their dedicated customers with discounts, free delivery or private events creating customer loyalty, which is worth its weight in gold. By letting the customers know that your price includes more than what they think they're paying for you can gain their loyalty over time. Those wineries that have marketing savvy know to price their products for a lasting customer relationship, which is preferable to a one-time transaction. They create different categories of pricing that motivate customers to do more business with them but also save money over the long term. Some wineries will bundle their products by adding additional products, think gift basket or buy one bottle and get one at a reduced price. By doing so they may not have to lower their pricing but the image of getting a deal remains.

An effective pricing strategy should have as its first priority the stability of the product to maintain sales. You don't have to look any further than gasoline prices and airfares that can fluctuate daily to know that there is nothing more irritating to the consumer than not having price stability. For a foreign company maintaining a stable price structure will not only be required by your distributors, especially in light of currency fluctuations, but may determine where the product will be manufactured and how the product will be shipped. Transportation costs, customs duties along with country tariffs can make a difference in your pricing and can affect whether you are profitable or not. The more you can stabilize your manufacturing and supply chain costs the better off you will be. Once you have these factors under control then the focus should be on controlling your competitor's response to your pricing actions. Planning ahead for a change in your competitor's pricing you would need to respond quickly and efficiently to their actions. This should be done while maintaining the loyalty of your established customers.

The advantages of being represented in any market is that you have the ability to consistently review your customer base and make any market and pricing changes fairly quickly. Domestic companies have the economies of scale where their products can be produced on a larger scale with less costs. Foreign companies have the ability to gain product recognition, provide a high level of service and still make inroads into the market. These companies tend to be the ones that have removed unnecessary operational costs, are incisive in their decision making and flexible in their pricing strategy. I would also suggest having product warranties or guarantees, which can help a foreign manufacturer prove that they stand behind their product's quality by offering the same warranties as domestic companies. In the U.S., unlike in other parts of the world, the product must live up to the expectations of the buyer, if not the product can be returned. Being new to the market I would suggest that you offer a guarantee beyond industry norms.

Winning the Price War

When a foreign company enters larger, sophisticated markets and begins acquiring market share, eventually it will become noticed by its competitors who in response to the entry will try to eliminate their opposition. The advantage you have as a foreign company is as long as you remain under their radar they will believe that you pose no immediate threat. The more you can stay adaptable to the market the greater chance of success you will have against your competition. As Charles Darwin noted, "It is not the strongest of the species that survives, nor the most intelligent that survives. It is the one that is the most adaptable to change."

To sustain a growth position requires both sufficient funding to maintain operations and pinpointed marketing programs to gain sales and market share. Underfunded companies without the appropriate market entry strategy and operational savvy will not be able to compete and will close. History has shown that companies that are preoccupied with their traditional rivals are blind to the risk from disruptive, lower cost competitors either domestic or foreign. The Japanese were able to gain a foothold into the American automobile market in the 1970s because U.S. automakers were not focused on building small compact cars. They should have paid attention to both Honda and Toyota who were gradually increasing their product lines to respond to the American consumer and in the process increased the quality and service of their cars. The result is that these companies are better prepared to absorb the market share of those automobile companies that have either closed or are floundering providing them with a stronger customer base to grow in the future. There is also the factor that as more companies go out of business prices for those remaining tend to increase.

The main reasons that price wars occur are:

- Competition between commodity products

- New companies trying to enter an established market

- Few competitors in the market where price is the only differentiator

- Over-production of products, flooding the market

- Predatory pricing where companies will deliberately price their products to eliminate others in the market

Most companies when entering a new market struggle with how to set prices on their products and services. Out of concern that customers may find their prices too high most will set their prices low to first gain traction in the market. Markets tend to go in cycles from a seller's market to a buyer's market as demand increases or decreases relative to supply. In a seller's market characterized by high demand there tends to be more buyers than sellers resulting in higher prices. To fulfill the need, manufacturers tend to be orientated to increasing supply through growing their production capabilities. Product differentiation in a seller's market is not necessary because of the limited competition. Usually to handle demand the manufacturer will try to increase production in the hopes of obtaining a greater profit for the company. A shortage of products in demand will usually make the consumer compete for a product thereby increasing their willingness to pay a higher price.

In a buyer's market, which has more sellers than buyers, the abundance of product has manufacturers competing for consumers, thereby reducing their prices to hold market share. Low prices result when the seller becomes focused on gaining customer specific information so they can offer them a lower cost bundled solution instead of individual costly products. This strategy is used by AT&T and cable companies to good effect.

With a foreign company trying to enter a market there are usually severe competitive pressures resulting in the buyer having the power in negotiating the price. New companies try to differentiate themselves from the huge selection of local competitors based on product price.

With globalization the increase in the number of companies doing business in foreign markets has grown faster than the demand for their products. This growth in companies provides the buyer a greater choice of what to choose thereby putting downward pressure on prices.

The reality is that unless you are Wal-Mart, being the low price leader maybe the worst thing you can do to your business. By lowering your price you increase the chance that your business might fail because it will take more capital for production to cover expenses. Consumer buying patterns and strategies tend to follow income. The best strategy is to be attractive to the segment that has a high income and then set your price in the range they would expect to pay. Prospective customers with high incomes will not shop the low price leader. They still want good value for their money. They buy quality because they can afford it.

The difficult part about being the high price, high quality leader is you have to work to keep your customers and it will require expert sales skills to attract and maintain them. Once you attract them, they will be more demanding because they chose you on the promise of quality products and service and now you must deliver.

If the demand for your products is low, you need to get better at sales and marketing your product. A lack of sales is seldom caused by price. It is almost always a problem with ineffective marketing or selling.

Collaborate and Improvise

The question I am frequently asked is how does a strong social and business network help eliminate a competitor's predatory pricing? The answer is best stated by Charles Darwin who said, "In the long history of humankind those who learned to collaborate and improvise most effectively have prevailed." Companies that have developed and nourished a strong network of supporters and influencers have the ability to move the market. These people can come from social media or from traditional industry customers, alliances or partners and are in a better position to support you than those that do not have connections. The industry rule-of-thumb that 20% of your resellers will generate 80% of your revenue applies equally well to all potential supporters and influencers no matter what media. This means that you will spend a lot of time working with these groups and most will not provide a return. But the ones that do can make a crucial difference in your revenues.

Industry leaders tend to take an offensive position by developing a lower cost business mentality instead of trying to differentiate their products from their competition. While many companies focus on selling higher margin products, others have successfully focused on doing the opposite ruthlessly pushing for higher turnover to increase their operating margins. You only have to look at the success of Wal-Mart and Costco to see how this works. Your ability to get the price you want depends to a large extent on how your customers perceive the value of your product. Having a wide community of influencers who can promote your products will enhance your customer's perception of value. With the ability to comparison shop using the Internet, consumers tend to become more aware of alternative, copycat and secondary brands—those products made by name manufacturers but packaged under a different brand name.

Then there are those companies that lose focus or dilute their marketing message by making it difficult for others to understand what they are trying to provide to the customer. This is especially prevalent with foreign engineering based companies that have technology whose value is difficult to explain in monetary terms. Having an inconsistent message will result in customers being unsure of what they are getting for the money. When the customer is unsure or has doubts about what they are getting, they are hesitant to buy. Sales experts will tell you that you never quote price without a value statement. I would agree with that assertion but you need to go further to differentiate yourself from the competition by wowing the buyer. This can be done by using a multimedia approach to your Web site or the use of innovative design of both the product and packaging. It all comes down to presentation.

The consumers in the United States are divided into two categories, those who buy on value whether real or perceived and those who buy on price alone. Help your customers get maximum value at the lowest price and you can win both to your product offering.

The Influence of the Media

The United States is a media driven market. The buying public is influenced by movies, television, print, or the Web, which reflects the cultural norms for the society. Technology companies such as Cisco Systems, Motorola, Apple Computer, and others pay a premium to place their products on television shows and in the movies just to get visibility. E-cards that are either free or purchased on Web sites and transmitted via the Internet are replacing traditionally mailed greeting cards among Internet user. These Web-based greeting cards tend to be interactive or multimedia, which in many cases can be customized for the buyer. As text, instant messaging and other forms of online communications flourish, the traditional postal service will continue to decline. The media has a greater influence on numerous demographic segments of society than ever before. Just travel to an American shopping mall during the December holiday season and you will notice that more people have used the Web to explore the products that they are interested in and going to the retailer to receive discounts on those selected products. Having a knowledgeable store clerk to assist you rather than merely to transact the purchase becomes harder to find every year. Many clerks are representatives of the brands being carried and are not store employees. The downside for business in this new media age is that if there is a problem with a product or the customer had a poor shopping experience then their response to the situation can be immediately posted to their networks through the use of blogs, news reports, Twitter, and instant messaging.

A recent example of the power of the media occurred when Chinese-made products such as baby formula, wallboard, dog food, and toys were found to be defective, which prompted people to communicate this news instantly through media outlets. Not only did these reports make the newspapers and television news but word of the problem was disseminated on blogs, Facebook, and YouTube. As social media and the Internet mature, different methods of marketing and sales will have to be developed to accommodate the changing consumer behavior and the technology used.

Market Factors

Not understanding the expectations of your target market and the way they want you to sell to them can ruin a perfectly good opportunity. I was invited to a forum attended by a 300 member delegation from Vietnam to promote the investment benefits of their country to U.S. business. They were looking for primary U.S. businesses in Silicon Valley such as HP, Oracle, and others to invest in their country. There were very few leading U.S. companies in attendance during the presentation and most were not in a position to buy what this delegation was trying to sell. The lack of U.S. response may have been due to the delegation forgetting to take into consideration that there are other buying criteria besides price and value that may influence the consumer. These factors include:

- **Market timing**—Where does the product fit within the market? Early, mid, or late stages.

- **Customer timing**—Is the customer ready for your product or service?

- **ROI**—What is the return on investment for selecting the product?

- **Financial**—Are the funds available or have they been budgeted for the purchase of the product?

- **Internal political risk**—Can the buyer minimize the political risk if the decision is wrong?

- **Executive management**—Can the purchaser sell the purchase internally to their executive management?

- **Advocacy**—Is there an advocate to help sell the product in the organization?

- **Buyer's goals**—What is in it for the purchaser if he should buy the product?

- **Sales pitch**—Was the sales pitch compelling?

- **Sales rapport**—Has the salesperson built good rapport with the purchaser?

It was apparent from the outset that the representatives of the Vietnam government and their attending companies were not prepared or trained on how to market and sell to the U.S. corporate customer. This was noticeable from the quality of the presentations to the delivery of their speeches; they really did not take the time to understand the audience's requirements. This delegation, for all the money that was spent on travel, food and the event itself was unfamiliar with the sophisticated workings of a more mature and established market. Cultural differences played a major role in how these Vietnamese CEOs presented their company's value proposition as well as how they interacted with Americans. Many of these Vietnamese companies behaved in similar fashion to their European counterparts that tend to be hierarchical and autocratic in their corporate structure and decision making processes. They tend to focus on direct selling to the CEO of the targeted company unaware that this may be the incorrect level of decision maker. What they don't realize is that in American companies the decision making process is more diversified and requires a greater consensus. Depending on the expenditure, the CEO may never be involved in the purchasing decision and the time trying to get to the CEO level may be time wasted on their part. Every sales representative would like to sell to at the "C" level but many product category decisions are made lower in the organization. You have to know the decision making process and what the criteria are for each company and focus your tactics appropriately. That did not occur at this event.

The seller, in more mature markets should be selective about who they take on as customers. I met a CEO of a mid-sized foreign company that wanted to sell his product line to one of the largest retailers in America. After working the account for over a year trying to get his products into this retailer he finally had his product accepted. Within nine months of his products acceptance his company was out of business. This small manufacturer could not meet the demands of the retailer and he wasn't able to get the capital needed in time to expand his business to meet his retailer's commitments. In the twenty-first century, making money will have as much to do with the customers you don't take on as those that you do. Don't expect your customer to figure out what your product can offer them. You have to tell them!

Making a Profit in a Commodity World

Globalization has made products from many countries more alike than different. It has also ushered in the age of low-prices by plummeting costs and making the Web's ability to operate from anywhere in the world the norm. For a company to make a profit in this environment they will have to proactively manage the process of commoditization by putting marketing before sales. This is done through the use of different media and networking sites to make the product visible while giving the customer multiple ways to purchase the product; all the while focusing on streamlining operations and reducing costs. Marketing's goal is to capture the attention of your prospective customers while assisting them with their decision making process. This has been demonstrated during the past decade with new technology products such as cell phones and PCs that first sold to businesses but now go directly to the consumer market. This results in manufacturers reducing their need for a large sales force. This reduction is a change from the past where manufacturers would send in a trained salesperson to demonstrate their product to the customer. For most small to medium sized businesses the start of the sales process begins over the Web and is concluded either by phone or in person. Except for their key accounts, manufacturers have laid off their highly paid sales force and outsourced the customer contact to their partners and distributors to manage.

One factor that has not changed in globalized business, whether conducted through the social media or through traditional business dealings is that personal relationships matter. Personal connections are as important today as ever. Connecting with people on Facebook, LinkedIn, YouTube, video conferencing or face-to-face all play a role in expanding a business into a new market. This is why you see the transition of focused roles in the organization becoming blurred. You now have bank tellers with sales goals and retail salespeople at Abercrombie and Fitch doubling as live models for their clothing line.

Staying Vendor-of-Choice

Once you have won a new account the pressure will be to maintain your pricing and to provide quality service and support. You can't afford to accept business that will not make a profit but customers will try to push you to keep your prices low, shrinking your margins. Selecting the correct mix of manufacturing capability and available supply chain options can either position a product as high-margin value-added or a low-margin commodity. Finding the balance will be important as there is a certain point in the process where a profit can no longer be made. The decision needs to be made regarding the best place to manufacture the product considering labor, transportation, export and import costs as well as the availability of capital. To make money under these circumstances requires managing your cost structure. To do this requires constant vigilance to new and innovative ways to increase productivity while reducing your costs of operations. For any company it is never wise to assume that you have the same cost structure as your competitors. In most cases you will not have that luxury because most of your competitors will be local to the market and have an established support network.

Once your technology product has been bought and is embedded at your customer's location, don't assume that you can then raise your pricing. I have seen too many customers remove equipment because the vendor changed their prices or service commitments and even though they may not want to change vendors they did so based on lower price and better service from another supplier. U.S. retailers such as Wal-Mart, Costco, Safeway, Target, and others are constantly putting pressure on their vendors to hold back price increases and replacing them when their price structure goes too high. There are three pricing questions for a foreign manufacturer to consider when dealing in this environment:

1. How much can be charged over the competition before your customers consider switching?
2. How low do your competitors have to price their products before they can challenge your position?
3. What would your competitor have to do in order to lower their cost structure enough to offer that price?

When you are the dominant supplier faced with a competitor who is offering a lower price to gain a foothold in the market, you may have to reduce your expenditures to a point but still make your margins.

Competitive Constraints

The United States as well as other countries has established laws and regulations regarding the restriction of trade and competition between businesses. The purpose of these laws is to promote a level playing field by prohibiting any abusive behavior by a company that holds a dominant position in the market or is using anti-competitive methods that would create a monopoly. These practices could include predatory pricing, tying, price gouging, refusal to deal, and many others. Violations of the law can result in both civil and criminal penalties as well as damage awards. U.S. and foreign governments cooperate by sharing evidence and prosecuting international antitrust cases.

These laws were established to ensure the free flow of competition by preventing a distributor from limiting the ability to freely sell or license your products. A manufacturer may suggest a resale price to the distributor but the distributor must have the ability to depart from these prices and to establish their own. Price isn't the only consideration because the law also includes non price restraints. It is illegal to restrain trade by exclusive distributorships or dealing provisions that contain language stating that the distributor cannot carry competing products. It is also illegal to require territorial limitations that ban sales outside an established territory or ones that tie the sale of a product to the purchase of another. Tying is against U.S. antitrust law when a supplier is unable to show a legitimate justification to tie a well performing product with one that isn't.

Robinson-Patman Act

The Robinson-Patman Act prohibits a seller from selling comparable products to different buyers at different prices unless they offer the same discount structure to all the buyers. The legal way is to offer the same pricing structure to all buyers and make promotional allowances and services available to all competing parties. This requirement includes advertising, promotional literature, sales and marketing assistance, and other payments and services in connection with the resale of the product.

To stay on the safe side and to avoid any possible litigation it is best to check with a U.S. attorney familiar with competitive pricing issues as you develop your distributor and customer agreements.

Positioning

If your business is like most businesses, you have your share of competition. Even small market niches are usually served by at least two to three competitors. In stable markets, each of these companies owns and defends a segment of the market. Even for those companies that are prospering it is rare for management to be satisfied with their market niche. Large companies want to take over smaller niches and small companies want to get a piece of the bigger market.

A clear, credible, and well executed positioning strategy is the foundation of your company's long-term market success. The objective of a positioning strategy is to identify the market segment you can own, in which you can build and defend a portion for long-term market leadership. A distinctive selling proposition and a clear competitive advantage will make it easier for you to gain investors, secure distribution channels, and win sales over your competitors.

Competitive Analysis

Emerging growth companies need to demonstrate an understanding of their competitors in their market entry strategy and tactics. Knowledge of the competitive landscape is important to determine how to position your company and product in the marketplace. It enables you to distinguish between competitor and complementary partners. Knowledge of competitor sales and promotional tactics is useful in deciding upon and differentiating your own.

New markets offer an array of opportunities for manufacturers willing to take the risk. Competition in established markets is fierce and hurdles have to be overcome, but a new silk road awaits those who can enter successfully. Due to the vast influx of immigrants to our shores, Americans in this age of globalization have ignored the advice of our third president, Thomas Jefferson when he professed that "I have come to a resolution myself as I hope every good citizen will, never again to purchase any article of foreign manufacture which can be had of American make be the difference of price what it may." Although he might feel differently today knowing the large numbers of foreign companies that have relocated their operations to the United States.

For many around the world there is an underlying concern regarding the changes that are occurring from increased competitive globalization. I have heard from foreign trade commissioners that globalization is affecting the economic and political stability of their citizens and their competitiveness as a country. I have witnessed that equitable trade policies differ between Europe and Asia. Nevertheless, I have also seen that these governments are perfectly willing to continue transferring technology overseas in the hope of opening new markets for their country's products while providing their businesses with low-cost labor and production. With advances in transportation, communication, and information technologies, these governments and chamber organizations to curb this situation for their country's businesses are putting very little effort forth.

The few organizations that have good intentions are limited to how much assistance they can provide their fellow citizens. In most cases these organizations operate under the guidelines that have been in place because the end of World War II. They are measured on the ability to grow their membership, the number of events created and the overall number of attendees participating. Most organizations continue only to perpetuate themselves, oblivious to the new operating methods brought about by technological changes that have occurred in communications, computers, networking, and supply chain logistics.

I was surprised that these organizations want to charge foreign companies to join them even though these companies are their best resource to assist their membership in entering new markets. By doing so they limit the association and experience that can be gained by having a free flow of information. Unlike the focused networking groups on LinkedIn or Ecademy, they tend to focus more on social gatherings instead of creating viable businesses.

9 The Dragon, the Tiger, and the Eagle

A man without a smile should not open a shop.
Chinese Saying

The emergence of India and China as global economic powers has changed the nature of global trade not only in Asia but worldwide. The economic growth from these two countries' trade and export dominance affects how other emerging businesses from different countries will enter new global markets, especially that of the United States. Their mixture of low wages, specialized work, regional supplier networks, and focused export only polices has enabled China to become the global economy's low-cost supplier and India the outsourced software development capital. Unlike India, China has planned slowly and meticulously for global business expansion by adopting a strategy of market entry that focuses on key foreign markets. This is similar to what Japan and South Korea accomplished in the 1980s and 90s. Once a beachhead was established for their companies they moved forward by acquiring greater market share and brand recognition as they expanded outward to other parts of the world.

China's approach differs by first entering the U.S. with their products and second acquiring existing U.S. companies for their brand recognition. This strategy is a significant change from what originally began as a foreign designed contract manufacturing operation. The strength of this strategy by China is that they not only have kept the manufacturing of the foreign designed products but also are using modified designs to manufacture products as their own brands. This affects U.S.-Chinese joint ventures because the Chinese partner can use the relationship with their multinational U.S. counterpart to enter multiple global markets.

China is implementing new strategies for their country's small to medium sized businesses to enter foreign markets not by imitating Western methods but by developing new methods and processes to conquer these markets. Chinese companies do not have to compete for the distribution channels because they have ridden the coattails of their U.S. partner. These tactics create a huge advantage that would not be available to non-Chinese companies. Chinese companies are breaking into new markets particularly in the higher value segments such as alternative energy, computers, and automobiles where they can gain market intelligence by being in close proximity to their customers and to vital innovation centers. Non-Chinese companies will have to do likewise to make inroads into these markets if they want to stay competitive. In the meantime, while the world's largest economies have slowed; emerging economies are expanding at a rapid pace. American small and medium sized businesses, which have traditionally been focused on domestic growth, have discovered exporting as a way to grow their revenues. The strategic priorities for them are the emerging markets of China, India, Brazil, and Russia.

China's business juggernaut is focused and moving forward with their twenty-first century model for doing business—a one-world concept geared to penetrating the American and the well-guarded markets of the European Union for the purpose of profit and influence. In order for non-Chinese companies to enter the Chinese market they must be willing to share their technical knowledge and intellectual property, which is not reciprocated.

China prefers to do business with foreign companies in two ways. The first more traditional way is to establish equity joint ventures with these foreign manufacturers who want to enter the Chinese market. Establishing a joint venture provides the foreign company the following:

- The ability to utilize their existing manufacturing infrastructure

- The desire to build new operational capabilities

- The facility to gain the knowledge and practices of the Chinese market

- A preferential way of handling market entry for their products

In return for the opportunity to enter the Chinese market, the foreign manufacturer will provide the technology, manufacturing know-how, marketing experience, and in many cases the assistance to open their own markets to the joint venture. However, providing this information and assistance to the Chinese company they may be paving the way for possible competition between these businesses in the future.

The second method for entry into the Chinese market is designed for the foreign retailer wanting to enter the market by establishing a wholly owned foreign enterprise. The world's leading retailers and suppliers have focused on China with the intention of acquiring a billion new consumers with increasing disposable incomes in which to sell their goods and services. These wholly owned foreign enterprises (WOFE) make market entry easier for this segment of companies. The WOFE works well for those companies who want a rapid entry into the market to begin to position and sell their products.

A WOFE would apply to small foreign chains with plans for less than thirty outlets and can be either a wholesaler or enterprise business and is either geared to franchising or direct selling. Many foreign companies such as H&M, Zara and Uniglo use this method to sell their products both online and in stores. In China, Web-based shopping has grown to handle more of the middle-income population, the fastest growing segment. With the growth of this segment, China has become the world's largest cell phone market and has surpassed any other country in the number of Internet users.

These 360 million Internet users[6] or "Netizens" as they are referred to use social media and blogs to stay informed about areas of interest to them. As in the West, they learn about and select products based on the influence of their social network. Manufacturers catering to these users have developed products that are both tangible and intangible in value. Where tangible value is geared to the product design, price, and quality, the intangible focuses on the shopping experience, status, and the brand image.

The middle-income Chinese consumer, like their Western counterparts are looking for quality in the products they purchase. They want the assurance that if the product breaks they can get it repaired, replaced, or receive a refund.

In the past the Chinese have been know as a culture of savers. This trend is gradually changing as the younger affluent individuals are looking forward to participating in the "good life" by going after the latest fads thereby increasing their status with their peer groups. Chinese consumption is estimated at 35% of the economy while Europe is 55% to 65% and the United States is from 70% to 72%.[7] As in the United States and Europe these younger Chinese believe that style and taste are just as important as brand identification.

For the foreign manufacturer a WOFE eliminates the need for a joint venture but is restricted to specific products and methods of doing business. As a Chinese legal entity you are able to hire workers as long as you abide by existing labor laws. The joint venture provides a foreign company the ability to purchase land and build factories.

A joint venture in China is particularly challenging. Foreign companies face a more difficult approval process and need to make an appealing case for the joint venture. Once approved a joint venture is usually limited in time from between thirty to fifty years. Share holdings in a joint venture are usually non-negotiable and cannot be transferred without approval from the Chinese government. Investors are restricted from withdrawing capital during the life of the agreement. There are specific requirements for the management structure of a joint venture. A minimum amount of capital must be contributed by the

---

6. Internet World Stats
7. International Monetary Fund

foreign company while no such restriction applies to the Chinese partner. There are additional restrictions on the joint venture that are not imposed by other countries looking for foreign investment. The deal process is fluid and requires a willingness to adjust the terms and conditions of each specific deal. Many companies have been hesitant to move into the Chinese market because of involuntary knowledge transfer. Many foreign companies have found that moving their production to China to cut costs has resulted in the development of competitors using much of the same technological knowledge to undercut them in the market.

Wholly owned foreign enterprises are similar to the market entry options used in the United States but with more restrictions. You will still have to resister the company and the brand trademark but you can sell directly without any foreign agents.

The Chinese have become very astute in product development and have a better understanding of the business world outside of their boarders than most foreign companies have of the Chinese. Their irreverent, can-do attitude is duplicated in only a few countries worldwide. Like the Israelis, Americans, and Indians, the Chinese are fearless and extremely confident in their business dealings. The Chinese are mastering the skills usually found in non-Chinese companies such as marketing, innovation, branding, and effective management skills as they bring their operations in line with international business practices.

Building a brand from scratch is a challenging task for any company. In many cases Chinese retail manufacturers have traveled overseas to register their companies and develop their products with the sole purpose of coming back to the China as a foreign brand hoping that the company's acceptance will be better than if they had remained at home. These companies understand that they don't have the luxury to wait before expanding into other markets unlike non-Chinese companies have done in the past by gradually entering new markets with their products. Buying foreign companies for their established brands is a short cut in their pursuit for competitive global market advantage.

The Chinese domestic market like the United States and Europe is not one market but made up of many local markets. The Chinese population is made up of fifty-six ethic groups with the Han comprising ninety-one percent of the population. Where local manufacturers and retailers once held dominance in their markets, today they are finding themselves under pressure from both foreign and domestic companies striving to gain market share. This situation is no different from in the United States where local manufacturing has gone overseas and big box stores have moved in displacing the locally owned smaller retailers. As China continues to open to the world its low cost and vast manpower reserves with the technological savvy and capital infusion from the West it is on its way to becoming the world's largest manufacturer.

China and India are developing a close affinity with the other peoples of Asia. China is developing closer economic ties with India, Japan, South Korea, and Taiwan in its goal to expand its market influence worldwide. India is developing closer economic ties with its immediate neighbors as well as Europe and the United States. Companies anticipating global expansion need to be aware that China and India together account for approximately forty percent of the world's population and will drive economic expansion in the twenty-first century. These countries believe that the future trend across Asia will be that financial and economic power will shift from the West to the East in their favor.

As the markets in China and India grow over the next decade, their companies that have successfully operated abroad will play a central role in shaping the products and services to fit the tastes of their own domestics markets. They will also bring new knowledge, technologies, and methodologies back to their countries replacing their reliance on western companies.

The Tata Group based in India has operations in every principal international market and is investing in overseas assets such as Tetley, Corus, and Jaguar Land Rover all formerly United Kingdom companies. They also own Daewoo Commercial Vehicles from South Korea, NatSteel from Singapore, Tyco Global Network, and General Chemical from the United States.[8] The Indian consumer tends more than their

---

8. Tata Group

Western counterparts to maintain established brands. For many British companies that have long been out of business their brand is now owned by Indian manufacturers whose products are still alive and well and remain popular with the Indian consumer.

There are differences in the current business environment between India, China, and the United States. The challenge of mutual understanding is great. All three countries have different approaches to business that often appear incompatible. These deep cultural differences in management styles, business priorities, and negotiation methods all take time to understand and to overcome. From an American viewpoint the issues in dealing with both India and China can be summarized as follows:

- Partially opened market for foreign goods and services

- Limited market sophistication

- Limited legal structure especially with direct foreign investment and ownership

- Intellectual property issues

- Limited sales and distribution channels

- Language barriers

- Limited local venture capital opportunities

- Limited service support community: attorneys, marketing, advertising, etc.

- Supply chain issues including transportation and ports

- Banking issues

- Limited transparency in business dealings

- High rates of poverty in the country

- Demographics

As Chinese and Indian businesses establish a beachhead outside of their own countries and continue their migration to the United States, Europe, and other markets it becomes clear that there are advantages of moving into the American market. The United States is a sophisticated and open market with its economic growth being driven by large amounts of investment capital. America has always been driven by entrepreneurship. Its foundation was established on burgeoning enterprises from shipbuilding, printing, and textiles to high-tech services and retail that serve a local customer base. Because the end of World War II the United States has set standards for the way business would be transacted in many parts of Europe and Asia. These standards of conduct are easy to understand and are the basis of the legal framework for doing business with American companies. Americans and Indians put a high emphasis on networking both in person and through social media unlike the Chinese who have in the past placed there business dealings within their peer group, friends, relatives, and close associates. Americans tend to trust others unless given a reason not to. They tend to challenge common wisdom by questioning and observing all the while having the luxury of associating with a diversity of people. This is not always the case in China, where there is a high degree of suspicion of strangers.

Both China and India are limited in their market entry options and the number of channels that are available. Each of these countries has imposed barriers for foreign companies wanting to enter their markets. In most situations this has not been the case in the United States. In the financial realm, venture capital and global banking are expanding in both countries but are limited in comparison to the United States. China and India conduct their overseas business through direct sales to importers except for IT outsourcing. The U.S. conducts their overseas business using overseas affiliates rather than through the sales of exported goods from the United States. These affiliates typically will produce the product locally in the foreign country using local labor and facilities. This provides the U.S. manufacturer easier access to the local customer base.

China has developed a better physical infrastructure than India to support economic development and trade. They have funded electric power plants, a network of modern highways connecting primary cities, railroads, and a sophisticated telecommunications infrastructure. China has reduced their travel time for exported products by modernizing their port capacity focusing on containerized shipping, which India has yet to develop. China handles twenty percent of the world's container traffic. Using Hong Kong as a special administrative region, China has been able to deploy their financial systems and tax laws to expedite both trade with the mainland and the rest of the world. Hong Kong provides China with a large and sophisticated business support community, banking, and an advanced supply chain capability, which India is lacking. In many ways China's economic growth resembles the industrial growth that occurred in the United States during the late 1800s to the early twentieth century. Moving westward from the eastern seaboard; building railroads, steel mills, highways, and power plants to power the industrial growth of China in its quest for economic independence from their old way of life.

India also has deep business and cultural ties to the United States especially to Silicon Valley. Immigrants from India have founded technology startup companies and venture capital firms that have had a significant impact on the growth of high technology and other industries in the valley. However, for all its growth, India has begun to do reverse outsourcing because they don't have enough skilled workers locally to handle the explosive growth that is occurring back home. India is looking outward for support to help build their infrastructure especially their ports, electric power facilities, and the needed network of roads all required to support global business. Once this occurs India will be better positioned for competitive growth.

The social networking explosion that started in the United States on the Internet with Web sites such as Facebook and Twitter is now taking on a different dimension in countries like India where online Internet penetration remains low. India has 52 million personal computers in comparison to 500 million cell phone users[9] making it more feasible for social networking and marketing companies to use the cell phone to promote their messages than the computer.

Consumer purchasing habits are based on age, literacy, and culture, which will make a difference in how your potential partners and customers interact with you. You don't have to go overseas to see this play out. By visiting the corporate offices of Google you may glimpse these demographic and cultural changes that are taking place in

---

9. Wikipedia

American business. On the other hand, with the economic powerhouse of China emerging and influencing the way business is conducted in Asia, the trend of the future may lie with the methods used by China to conduct business. Either way, the influence of the younger, educated business executive will determine the methods used to conduct global business in the future.

Foreign companies need to understand the financial issues of the export and import regulations for the cost implications to them. Knowing the duties and tariff restrictions placed on goods from specific countries or categories of products can save you time and money. These duties and tariffs can make a difference on whether to venture abroad with your products or where to have them manufactured. A 1% to 2% duty may make a difference whether you will be profitable or not. It will also make a difference in which country the product is manufactured, assembled, or shipped from.

As demand for low-cost goods and services is increasing, manufacturers in China are having a difficult time absorbing the rising cost of labor, energy, and materials forcing them to look outside of China for lower cost areas to setup shop. Many of these Chinese companies have shut down their operations and others are forced to find new ways of production to stay competitive. This situation tends to commoditize products while the manufacturer's margins become razor thin and cost reductions are pushed down through the entire supply chain process. In many cases manufacturers are forced to modify their packaging or even redesign their products to maintain their margins. The other issue facing foreign companies wanting to enter the markets of India and China is the slew of potential substitute products or cheap knockoffs that will become available after you enter the market. It is difficult to avoid this possibility but a foreign manufacturer can begin selling directly to these customers online or through company owned stores as an alternative. Using the power of social media in these countries to drive product interest and sales may help in keeping tighter control on the brand and on your margins.

American companies, especially those that are not multinational corporations have to be aggressive players in these global markets. American companies still depend on the United States for the majority of their sales unlike those companies from small, more closed markets, which can't run on domestic demand alone and need to expand outward to continue making revenue. American and other western business cultures often appear incompatible with the Chinese way of doing business. Americans often see the Chinese as efficient, indirect, and even insincere. Americans see the Israelis and Germans as overly direct, aggressive, and in a rush to get things accomplished. The German culture is task- and time-oriented, which makes it difficult for them to establish business relationships outside of Germany. For rela- tionship-minded cultures such as those in Asia and India, social media is the perfect tool. Israelis and Indians actively join networking groups and associate freely with diverse people from other countries. For all cultures diversity has deep historic origins. Those who grasp how to navigate this diversity can develop thriving, mutually profitable, and satisfying business relationships. Americans need to see foreign markets not only as a place to source inexpensive goods but as an expanded home market.

Because World War II, Europe has taken a secondary role as a new product innovator due to being risk averse and cautious about launching into new markets. Even though the Euro united the different currencies it did little to create a single market. Unfortunately the Europeans have forgotten what French author and Nobel laureate André Gide professed, "One doesn't discover new lands without con- senting to lose sight of the shore for a very long time."

The United States and the European Union are open, established markets; India and China are only partially open. Both China and India lack the legal structure in the area of intellectual property rights. There remains political and economic risk for those companies that are con- sidering entering these markets.

As the markets in China and India expand, more of their domestic brands will become available on the global stage, making it more difficult for foreign manufacturers to compete. Presently the difficulty is minimal due to India and China not establishing copyright, quality control, or merchandise return policies. While Chinese and Indian companies have the local knowledge of their markets, China tends to have the leverage in the other Asian markets that global companies are seeking. The government of China seeks its global objectives following careful study, patience, and accumulation of knowledge about the operations of foreign markets. This of course is hindered by individual companies that introduce substandard products worldwide, damaging the reputation of Chinese manufacturing.

Heavy discounting is now occurring worldwide especially in the retail sector with the increase of international mega-stores such as Wal-Mart. Trying to bring a new product into the market on a test basis is almost impossible with retailers hesitant to keep large amounts of inventory on hand and constant pressure to keep prices low and quality high.

The Internet is one way to keep costs down and can increase the rate of which new products from around the world can enter both established and emerging markets. Whether through services such as Alibaba, Facebook, or YouTube, global market entry is changing. Every new social media market has to attract enough participants to make it worthwhile. What makes this media valuable for foreign companies is the access, user traffic from different countries as well as the time or stickiness that they spend on using these Web sites.

I was working with a computer company whose products were designed in Europe and manufactured in China. Prior to entering the U.S. market this European company knew who their competition was and how their products were to be positioned. They also knew the demographics of their potential customer base. However, they didn't have a grasp of the limited channels available for distribution of their product in America. Initially these products were being shipped airfreight from Europe to the United States at a reasonable wholesale price. In time their competitors began to reduce their prices under pressure from U.S. retailers. They were forced to rethink their transportation methods from Europe. To keep their prices competitive I worked with the manufacturer to redesign their outer packaging to reduce product weight and expense all the while searching for reduced cost transportation. We then reviewed their warehousing and fulfillment expenses and renegotiated the contract to reduce prices and to have just-in-time inventory on hand so their retailers did not have to maintain their own inventory. Their market success in the U.S. hinged on five changes they made. First they paid attention to the retailer's request, second to what their competition was doing, third to reducing their transportation costs, fourth to better inventory management, and fifth to quicker fulfillment. They made these changes in time for the crucial Christmas shopping season.

In the United States the start of the Christmas holiday shopping season begins in November, the Friday after the Thanksgiving holiday. The following Monday is known as Cyber Monday when people come back from the holiday and use this day to shop online for Christmas. It is estimated that 97 million people will go online to do their holiday shopping resulting in approximately one third of the population using the Internet. Retailers use their employees to help promote their Internet sales using these social media sites. With nine out of ten retailers having Web sites in the U.S. this medium is growing and replacing traditional methods of sales and marketing. As the markets of China and India expand they would do well to take advantage of online retailing to increase their sales opportunities.

10 Breaking Through the Barriers

Big goals can create a fear of failure. Lack of goals guarantees it.
Unknown

Much of the information we receive about doing business globally tends to be at odds with what is really occurring. Journalist who comment on the economy have little background or understanding of the subject matter on which they are reporting. I am a firm believer that director and playwright Ben Hecht was correct when he stated that, "Trying to determine what is going on in the world by reading newspapers is like trying to tell time by watching the second hand of a clock."

Newspapers and television hook their audience and make their sales by providing stories that promote fear, disaster, and uncertainty. Recognize that these reports are not necessarily to be believed; their agenda is only making money for themselves and has nothing to do with your success. You need to do your own research to validate what is reported as fact and determine if it applies to your business. "Destiny is not a matter of chance; it is a matter of choice. It is not a thing to be waited for, it is a thing to be achieved" stated the late William Jennings Bryan, one of Americas most popular speakers.

Business survival requires the ability to implement bold and creative ideas and to dominate potential rivals all the while generating revenue. Aggressive companies use a number of innovative approaches to gain market share from developing alliances to effectively using the marketing and sales channels that are available to them. They also tend to be more adaptable to changing their pricing structure and to re-focusing their marketing and sales efforts specifically to the target buyer. Real innovation involves companies that are willing to change their competencies and tactics in order to compete worldwide. Companies entering new international markets are apt to be more open, horizontal in their structure, and non-hierarchical in their deci-sion-making. They tend to be more efficient, focused, and accountable for their own success. By being more experimental and motivated they tend to transform the markets that they enter by pushing aside their competitor's products to win the struggle for the long run. What I have found that matters most for a foreign company's success in entering new markets are:

- Establishing and maintaining momentum

- Providing customers access to your products

- Making gains in market share to prove you are a serious contender

- Focusing on the customer's success

- Adapting quickly to new situations

- Providing quality service on every order

- Never compromising on what is good for the customer

Companies who realize that their home market is insufficient to support their company's growth have to look outward to expand. Few from their inception have the vision of expanding globally. I have seen the opposite with Israeli companies, which have an ingrained focus to be successful, meaning they have to be in the U.S. market. Then there are others that focus on their home market first; going global is only a secondary thought. However, before investing resources, you need to do the research because many companies do not have the products or services that appeal to the global market or cannot be successfully exported. Those companies that want to expand may run into capital issues that make it difficult for them to finance their operations to grow internationally. The infrastructure to help support these companies is as varied and diverse as the companies themselves. Most of these services whether government or private lack the vision and action needed by these neophyte companies as they endeavor beyond their home shores. What is lacking from these organizations may have been stated best by U.S. President Woodrow Wilson that "there are many voices of counsel but few voices of vision." Most of the companies that I have worked with would tend to agree with him. Market changes happen so rapidly it is difficult to predict accurately what products can sell despite better means of information we now have at our disposal.

Businesses, out of fear of making the wrong decision spend hour upon hour analyzing and reviewing the data, options, and alternatives without making a decision. Unfortunately a company will wait for their fear to subside before taking action. It is not necessary to get rid of fear in order to take action and most successful companies have found a way to use these fears to their advantage. They believe that any decision is better than no decision and one that can expand their revenues is worth the risk. These CEOs have learned more from taking action than from endless evaluation of the options available to them. Making the wrong decision or loosing face prevails in so many cultures that even if the risk is mitigated and all the data is in their hands before taking any action they still are hesitant to move forward. Unlike in the U.S. these executives fear what their managers, staff, family, or society in general will say if they are perceived as having failed. The only dif-ference between those who succeed in overcoming their fears and those who don't is that successful people act in spite of their fear, doubt, and worry.

Funding Sources

Most early and mid stage entrepreneurial companies require capital to both grow their company and to expand into global markets. Entering a new market requires sufficient capital to establish a presence, build product recognition and to maintain the daily operations of the company. Competition for funding is fierce and requires a well thought out business strategy prior to approaching any of the sources available. Most early stage or first time entrepreneurs know about the venture capital route to funding and assume that this is the best means available to them. For those outside of the United States who don't receive local investment it becomes more difficult to get American or other investors interested in the company and its products. If they do receive local investment it is usually insufficient for global expansion and will require further investment for development.

Sources of Financing

There are two methods of financing commonly used to start or expand a company. The first is equity financing, which is an ownership stake taken in the company by an investing party, usually in the form of common or preferred stock and can come from:

- Your own resources, family, and friends

- Business acquaintances

- Angel investors

- Venture capitalists

- Joint venture partners and strategic investors

The second method is debt financing when a company raises money by bonds, loans, and other financial instruments. In return for lending the money, the individuals or institutions become creditors and receive a promise that the principal and interest on the debt will be repaid. Debt financing can come from:

- Banks

- Finance and leasing companies

- Suppliers or customers

- Government grants

Either equity or debt financing can be successfully used to expand a company into a new market. When considering either form there are multiple sources that can be approached to try to secure the necessary funding.

Equity Financing

For equity financing there are five stages of capital traditionally used by entrepreneurs to start their companies.

Stage one or seed financing usually comes from family and friends or angels and is the capital used to purchase an equity-based interest in a new or existing company. Seed capital is usually quite small, less than $1 million because the venture is still in the conceptual stage.

Stage two is the capital provided to expand marketing and meet the growing working capital needs of the company, which does not have positive cash flow. The goal of the investor is to place experienced managers in an environment with a high probability for success. This may be with the oversight and experience of the investor. These funds are usually in the $5 million to $30 million bracket.

Stage three or multiple funding rounds come from venture capitalist in a series of preferred stock. Series A Preferred Stock is the first round of stock offered during the early stage by the venture capitalist. Series A preferred stock is convertible into common stock in certain cases such as an IPO or the sale of the company. Later rounds of preferred stock are called Series B, Series C and so forth. Third stage capital is provided to a company that has begun product production and basic marketing and is used for market expansion, acquisitions, product development, etc.

Stage four or mezzanine financing is late-stage venture capital, usually the final round of financing prior to an IPO. Mezzanine financing is for a company expecting to go public usually within 6 to 12 months and is to be repaid from proceeds of public offerings. Because there is a lot of risk involved for the lender or investor the interest rate is much higher than a regular loan. Mezzanine financings can be completed through a variety of different methods. The basic forms used in most mezzanine financings are subordinated notes and preferred stock.

Stage five, the Initial Public Offering, is the first sale of stock by a private company to the public.

To minimize the possibility of financial loss, venture capitalists mitigate their risk by investing in more than one company for each fund. Usually the average is ten companies per fund. Just like playing the roulette table in Las Vegas these individuals place their bets on multiple companies trying to reduce their losses while expanding their winnings. By expanding the funds they raised and investing in more than one company, their potential for loss becomes minimal because they now have safety in numbers. They are hedging their bets by safe-guarding that at least one or two of the ten companies they invested in will hit the target and make money for their investors.

"No" Is Just Another Way of Saying "Yes"

There are stories of successful writers who were rejected by publishers time and again before one finally picked up their work and it became a best seller. Entrepreneurs and CEO's of startup companies looking for initial funding are regularly turned away by venture capitalists who are obsessed with market risk and the fear of not achieving a substantial return on their investment. These are the common problems that any new venture is likely to face in getting off the ground. It doesn't take a genius to point out the risk associated with an early stage venture or entering a new and foreign market. Venture capitalist for all their knowledge and resources fear missing an opportunity as well as the possibility of losing money to the investor fund. They fear that by turning down a company, this same company will go to a competitor and became successful. For the entrepreneurial company the words of General Douglas MacArthur stand out—"There is no security on this earth, only opportunity."

Finding Investors

There are sources of capital you may overlook and can be very valuable in assisting with your company's market entry and growth strategy. These sources can be your established or prospective suppliers and customers. If these sources are interested in your company and its products for use within their own company, then there may be a possibility that they might assist you not only with the financing of your operations but with your expansion. If you are first-to-market with a solution to a problem they are encountering, then it may be a strategic fit for them. Your customers are always looking for ways to differentiate themselves in the market and if your product can help them do that while providing them a good return on investment they may want to invest in your company. The investment can be an equity stake, a joint venture or any number of the opportunities previously mentioned. In most cases if the product is horizontal in nature going across multiple industries and not specializing in the customers industry then the opportunity may be more lucrative because noncompeting companies can purchase the product. Most of the suppliers and customers you will be dealing with may not think of this option. It may behoove you, if you are in need of capital, to bring this option up to them and to make them an offer of equity for their financial support. You never know what will come from it.

With the advent of the Web it is much easier to find funding sources. Venture capital companies will indicate the types of investments that they have made and the companies that they are invested in. Beyond the VCs there is a range of options from angel investor groups to investment bankers that should be explored. The general resources to find these potential investors are:

- Networking with industry executives

- Angel investor groups

- Venture capital associations

- Web research

- Investor Web sites

- Press releases and newspaper articles on who is investing

- Business newspapers, *Wall Street Journal, Financial Times*

- Industry associations

- Local banks

Still the best way to begin finding the necessary funds required for growth is through networking. The key is to be introduced to a particular funding source by someone who is both familiar with you and trusted for their business acumen by these investing parties. Whether bankers, angels, or VCs the parties know and trust each other for their ability to spot potential investment opportunities, it then becomes easier for you to get a face-to-face appointment. These trusted individuals can be anyone, but those who invest tend to focus on people who they work with and can count on. These can be lawyers, accountants, bankers, college professors or business colleagues that have had their companies funded in the past. Besides the traditional sources there is a plethora of options from government grants and loans to high worth individuals. The more you can network and meet these potential sources of capital the better off you will be.

What Investors Are Looking For

Silicon Valley investors have always sought after companies with ideas, products, and solutions to gain a good return on their investment. These astute investors will look for companies that have thought through their business model and can demonstrate that they have the five key ingredients for business success. These are:

1. A large addressable market
2. Potential growth for allowing new entrants to succeed in the market
3. A sustainable competitive advantage
4. A profitable business model
5. An experienced management team that can lead the company to success

An idea that inspires passion and interest will always be of interest to an investor. Mary Kay Ash founder of Mary Kay Cosmetics said it best, "A mediocre idea that generates enthusiasm will go further than a great idea that inspires no one."

The Ways to Network

The Internet and the use of social media will continue to play a vital role in business and will be refined as the needs of the participants change. For those companies exploring their options for market entry there remain the traditional non-electronic means of networking. Available to you are casual referral partners who you will meet on a daily basis and if asked can refer specific companies or individuals to you. Being new to the market, focus on what are call "power partners" or "power groups" that can work with you as a team to help break down barriers and make the appropriate introductions to potential customers and in-fluencers that can help your business grow. It takes time to meet, establish yourself, and build the trust necessary for these individuals and companies to work with you. In most cases you will have to do a lot of exploring before you find the right ones that provide mutual benefit.

Preparing for Success in the Face of Globalization

What will the future look like for the foreign business owner trying to enter the U.S. market in the next few years? Will the "American dream" still be available for foreign companies or will the situation change due to America's thirst to off shore more of their technology, skills, and capital to the emerging markets around the world? Will the migration offshore be the death of the American entrepreneur? If not, how do we prepare ourselves for continued success and survival in the face of the globalization onslaught?

Thinking about the future means asking tough questions and facing some harsh realities. To be forward looking requires the time and resources to anticipate global changes. This is accomplished by under-standing the basic trends, patterns, and behaviors that are occurring on the global stage. It is by observing what is occurring in India, China, Brazil, and other countries to determine how you proceed with your business in America.

Trying to determine future trade and consumer trends is difficult and time consuming. Planning for them requires moving away from immediate observation and news reports to grasp the long-term meaning of the situation. Will your venture be profitable or bleak? Imagine how Sherlock Holmes would look beyond the obvious to the underlying meaning of a given situation. If he had observed what everybody else did, he would not have been a successful detective. For you to be a successful detective you need to consider what will affect your business. How will you be helped by the means of distribution such as Internet sales versus free standing stores? Once this is decided upon what method of shipping would be most cost effective and what manner of fulfillment would reduce turn-around time and warehousing costs? Prior to the purchase you need to establish pricing in comparison to your competitors. Service and support including refunds and replacements will need to be addressed.

Looking ahead to the future, will your product be relevant? Is it destined to be the next iPhone or the Betamax? Obviously the younger generation will continue to communicate with their friends and use computers. However, how will they adapt your product to suit their needs and how would you change your product development and marketing strategy to respond? Will your products fit with other technologies that keep evolving?

The American entrepreneurial juggernaut is being challenged by individuals and businesses from countries such as Brazil, Israel, and South Korea that were once on the sidelines of innovation and commerce. These countries will continue to increase in economic power through their exports of more universally accepted products. In the future I see a gradual shift away from American created and designed technology products to those of other countries. We are seeing advanced security and green technology products from Israel, alternative energy products from Brazil, and unique consumer electronics and heavy industry products from South Korea. Their solutions are distinctive from those of American companies and in the future these countries will continue to be more inventive and exercise greater influence over global needs. This demonstrates that innovated products don't always come from highly sophisticated or advanced countries.

I believe that the "American dream" will be attainable for foreign companies in the foreseeable future even though American businesses still offshore many of their operations. I am seeing more interest by small and medium sized businesses who never thought of expanding beyond their regional influence are now taking advantage of the opportunities first nationally then internationally. Silicon Valley companies and other businesses throughout America are getting educated to what resources are available to them abroad in the way of technology, labor, manufacturing, and capital to assist them in expansion. This migration offshore will not be the death of the American entrepreneur as so many have predicted. We are seeing renewed interest in alternative energy, healthcare, medical technology, and software that is being funded and incubated in the U.S. The entrepreneurial spirit that built the steel town of Pittsburg, the automotive capital of Detroit, the textile industries of the American South will continue to flourish in the decades ahead. The difference will be that small business, despite the barriers presently imposed on them by our government will fight for survival or be replaced by another spirited entrepreneur.

Predicting trends provides the executive with a deeper understanding of the driving forces affecting business. The executive will migrate from a myopic local view to a more global focus as events around the world will have a greater influence on local markets. When analyzing the effects of globalization the most significant trends likely to affect the world can generally are represented by four categories where change will occur:

1. **Societal**—demographics, lifestyle trends, immigration patterns
2. **Economic**—industry changes, competitive forces, changes in the workforce
3. **Political**—legislative, regulatory, policy changes
4. **Technological**—innovations, uses, adaption rates

Each category in itself can bring forth opportunities. Preparing to face the challenges of globalization requires a mindset of long-term global thinking. This is a similar vision that America's founding fathers had for the country's growth and positioning in the world. The other benefits of preparing ourselves for globalization will inspire a sense of urgency about the future, which then will promote proactive leadership initiatives to stay competitive.

By postulating different views of where business is headed, you can gain a sharper sense of your present work environment. You don't want to limit your company's potential in today's competitive marketplace. To do this, you can take the following pro-active steps:

- Identify internal and external factors currently affecting your business's performance.

- Enroll employees and associates into a shared vision of the future.

- Create contingency plans to respond appropriately to external changes.

- Challenge long-held internal beliefs.

- Incorporate the effects of change into long-range planning.

It has been said that we are in the middle of the biggest industrial shift in 200 years. Not because the Industrial Revolution has so much disruption occurred in the foremost global economies. Politicians and economists now look to small and medium-sized business to create the jobs and supply the innovation that is gone in larger companies. Multinational corporations who have moved much of their production offshore are turning their domestic operations into high value-added niche operations. As businesses around the world realize that they have to go global to survive, they are transforming themselves from manufacturing to marketing companies and keeping only about 10%–15% of their total workforce in their home country.

Resulting from this shift in manufacturing to lower cost emerging countries, more individuals out of necessity are establishing their own companies. It is estimated that in America alone more than 500,000 entrepreneurs[10] are involved in launching their own companies. Other than in the United States, Japan, and China few countries have this type of entrepreneurial transformation.

To be able to compete globally the entrepreneur will need to imagine a variety of future possibilities and to act to sustain their competitive advantage in the face of these changes. It is difficult to obtain

---

10. U.S. Small Business Administration

information about what is occurring in other parts of the United States let alone the world in the application of new technologies and product development.

The ability to maintain market dominance is predicated on both creating and imagining future trends in order to get better odds on the future and then to use this information for your own competitive advantage. The fact that business today is complaining about the Wal-Mart affect on their business and cannot compete with the size and buying power of this global competitor is a good example. The current response by both business and local government is to try to keep these large global box store retailers out. Wal-Mart may be the first, but it will not be last market influence that will affect the global entrepreneur. Understanding what is occurring in key foreign markets is critical for a company to position themselves to handle future market changes quickly and efficiently.

The approach to determining the direction of global markets is based upon:

- Knowing your company's strengths and your strategic advantage in the marketplace. This becomes the baseline for future planning and measurement.

- Identifying both market forces and trends that may affect your product. This can include new disruptive technology, consumer buying patterns, media influences, and competitors.

- Focusing on market information for a product by narrowing down the product line to a specific business function.

Searching for the Trends of the Future

There are only a handful of nations where the general populous embraces an entrepreneurial culture and is cutting edge in innovative technologies. Throughout history we have found that these nations change and those who were leaders at one time such as Italy and France have given way to Israel, South Korea, and the United States. Today you can count which nations are driving innovation on two hands. Whether the trends for the future are in alternative energy, enhanced food production or green technology, foreign companies will established themselves in the American market in order to springboard out to markets worldwide.

Recently at a solar industry exposition and trade show in San Francisco, the foreign companies showing their latest in solar products were from China, Germany, and Spain. Of these, only the Chinese companies were seeking distributors and other resources to assist them in entering the U.S. market. After the show, most of the foreign companies that had participated packed up and went home and never tried to enter the market. The ones that set up shop in the U.S. were free to act upon preconceived assumptions about how globalization would be able to benefit them. By being in the market these companies will be in a better position to recognize opportunities as well as the warning signs in the market as they unfold.

Yet, creativity without any limits is total chaos. By defining a timeframe for each possible trend, what emerges is a range of choices that identify potential threats and opportunities over specific periods of time. Many of these choices will go unnoticed by traditional company management focused obsessively on the organization's present-day situation and quarterly profits. By highlighting future warning a sign such as what a competitor is doing or a change in legislation, a business can avoid surprises and be better prepared to adapt and act efficiently. New strategies derived from future planning have the potential to create distinct competitive advantages.

Forecasting where markets are trending, positions a business for better performance if the data collected is accurate and timely and that the company has the ability to act on it. That means effectively executing a four-stage process:

1. Information collection through the use of focused real-time data from market research worldwide, media reporting, seminars, as well as public data available on the Internet

2. Occurrence trending by using the collected data, to model and simulate future events

3. What-if analysis to help determine the best course of action under various scenarios

4. Implementation to take action on your insights and assumptions

Determining business trends and knowing the likelihood of events occurring is of no use unless the entrepreneur has the flexibility to adapt and take action. By doing so, this process also provides the benefit of inspiring a sense of urgency about the future, promoting proactive leadership initiatives while drawing employees and service providers into a shared vision of the future. The key is to be able to execute and deliver on the right objectives.

Chapter 10: Breaking Through the Barriers

11 The Doorway to the World

Capital will go where it is wanted and stay where it is well treated.
Walter Wriston

International trade and commerce is about competing for global dominance. Companies are struggling to determine how best to position themselves to survive the changing market dynamics brought on by globalization. The competitive landscape for technology companies requires an understanding of today's markets and consumer buying habits as well as the cultural dynamics driving behavior and market changes. This can be local, regional, national, or international in scope. The affects of globalized change have had a trickledown effect on most communities around the world. This is best exemplified by products from multinational manufacturers such as Apple Computer, Microsoft, Nabisco, and Coca-Cola selling in countries around the world. It is also seen with the expansion of products manufactured in China, Japan, and other Asian countries filling store shelves in Europe and America.

Entry into new markets has become easier than at any time in history. Emerging global trade is increasingly becoming a threat to those established firms who have had to change their methods of operations to compete with the influx of new companies and products from different countries that are entering their sphere of influence. The historic challenge for any business is to find new ways to grow product sales and increase market share not only in their local market but on an international scale. Technology entrepreneurs and venture capitalists understand that they have to have a global presence and are creating multinational companies even before they make their first dollar. The nature of work is flowing to where it is produced efficiently and for the lowest cost. In India and China local companies are gaining the skills and experience to compete against multinational companies and gain global market share for their products and services.

The pressing question for any emerging company in this environment is what work will flow to them and on what basis will they be able to differentiate themselves to compete. In a competitive world, advantage will increasingly be based on the ability to create new and exciting products, services, and business models that are unique, compelling, and based on customer value. Silicon Valley has taught us that there are regions in each country that drive economic activity and innovation.

Many twenty-first century service industries located in countries such as India, China, Israel, and Ireland are powering business growth with their technology in computers, software, pharmaceuticals, media, and biotechnology. These countries are in the process of passing those traditional heavy manufacturing countries such as Germany, Belgium, and Great Britain that have a substantial reliance on cars, machinery, and chemicals.

We see this trend today as businesses from around the world continue to outsource their manufacturing to lower cost countries, which in turn hurts the home country. As the economist Sylvia Porter noted, "The soundest rule to remember is that whatever is to happen is happening already." The underlying trends that have been affecting the market have been visible for more than a decade. Markets are efficient by nature and without outside intrusion they tend to be in a state of balance. Consumption depends on income and wealth depends on a thriving business environment. If business is profitable, personal income increases and that in turn will fund consumption.

It is generally ineffective to allow your local marketing company to promote your products outside your domestic market. It is extremely rare for a foreign marketing firm to excel anywhere other than in their home country. It requires a U.S. marketing and sales team who know the competitive environment and sales styles to represent you in the U.S. market.

The Benefits of Global Trade

Throughout the history of humanity, global economic trade has resulted in numerous benefits for those individuals, companies, and countries that did business in foreign lands becoming wealthy in the process. In the twenty-first century, aggressive companies looking to expand their revenue performance know full well the benefits of foreign trade. The advantages that are derived by their actions to enter new markets worldwide include:

- Increase product and service sales—exporting is a way to expand ones market and take advantage of demand generation for products around the world.

- Increase profits—once fixed costs are covered through domestic operations, export profits can grow very quickly increasing overall company revenues.

- Economies of scale—with a larger market base, the scale of production provides for better utilization of company resources.

- Reduce risk exposure—diversification into international markets avoids depending on a single marketplace during economic cycles.

- New market knowledge and appreciation—the global marketplace abounds with new products, ideas, business approaches, marketing and sales techniques.

- Skilled and educated workers—are now available in every country with the capability of having a 24/7 workforce.

- Lower production costs—from the cost of labor, utilities, transportation, real estate, and other resources.

- Incentives—provided by governments may be available for certain types of manufacturers to reduce company relocation and operational expenses and to make it more conducive to do business.

- Competitive awareness—the experience gained internationally will help keep a company competitive in the global marketplace and profitable domestically with new products.

- Additional revenue streams—global businesses tend to have multiple revenue streams from product sales, service, and support, which can augment cyclical and seasonal fluctuations in the home market.

The process of developing and managing a business is focused on the future. Yet, for all our understanding and knowledge we are limited in our abilities to predict the future. Then how do we forgo chaos and make sound decisions? The bottom line is that we do not know the consequences of the choices we make, but by preparation they should outweigh any negative outcomes.

In a global seller's market it doesn't matter if a country's products or the way they are produced differ significantly from those of another country. But in a buyers' market, as we are seeing today, when the money flow slows and competition becomes fierce, the lack of either strategic positioning or product value will force companies to battle it out solely on price. Unless a company has been lucky enough to have created an exceptional product or service such as the iPod, Bluetooth, BlackBerry, and the iPhone that people are waiting in line to buy or they are successful in their business and market development strategy like HP, Apple Computer, EBay or Google the result will be that eventually every company will end up in the same place—a niche market.

Innovative companies such as Apple, Toyota, and Oracle have demonstrated that to maintain their market position for the long term they will base their tactics for winning on customer value and flawless execution. These companies take full advantage of market timing, product trials, expert guidance, strategic and tactical planning that will eliminate errors and problems beforehand maximizing the potential for achieving a successful outcome. They also understand that to compete for global dominance they have to develop their products from the outset for the international market and to execute different tactics for market entry for each specific targeted country. Successful global companies have gained an understanding of the world around them and know how to exploit that knowledge to their advantage. Multinational companies that have gone offshore have already adopted a lean business model striving for the lowest cost structure. By automating operations, focusing on quality, relying on knowledgeable experts in the countries they are dealing with and providing inexpensive, quality customer support and service keeps them competitive.

Any company can now build the required infrastructure at low cost to support market development and sales while building their international supply chain for expanding their products and services worldwide.

Trust

As global trade expands and people from different countries and cultures begin to work more closely together trust becomes an essential factor for business to be transacted. People from different cultures don't always feel comfortable doing business with each other. There is a lack of synergy that hinders their ability to get things done. High levels of trust can enable better performance between parties, which will foster greater innovation and creativity. Building trust will take time especially with cultures that are more circumspect, whose people will not come right out and tell you what they are thinking. When the Japanese or Koreans say they will get back to you they may in fact really mean "no" to your proposition. Knowing how each culture does business is critical. In dealing on an international basis one needs first and foremost to maintain integrity whereby both parties are consistent in their actions, methods, and expectations. The foundation of mutual trust is built by open communication, shared respect, and goals with no personal agenda. Finally it is critical in all cultures to maintain confidence in your business dealings and to do what is right by both parties.

By establishing and building trust you will be able to expand the area of possibilities for your company and move negotiations along faster.

Tokyo Café

There are trend makers in every industry and new and innovative ideas are springing up in all corners of the world. I recently read in a business journal about a new café in Tokyo's Shibuya district where customers are required to register by cell phone and provide their personal information to receive "tokens" for items they wish to try at a sample bar. This method of promotion is more affordable for manufacturers than television or magazine advertising. If the customers are pleased with the experience they spread the word using the Internet.

The use of the Internet and social media networks has grown to the extent that business among its users is now conducted in new and more productive ways. The Internet has provided advantages to foreign companies by creating a new form of delivery for busy consumers anywhere in the world. During the end of the technology bubble in 2003 many of Silicon Valley's largest technology companies realized the power of the Internet and began to downsize their sales forces. This enabled their customers to have access to their marketing materials as well as encouraging them to make purchases directly from their Web sites. This has become more prevalent as more retailers are using the Internet to merchandise and sell products from their suppliers. Foreign companies can gain market share with new and innovative products, bypassing the traditional means of entry using this media. New competitors whether foreign or domestic will introduce disruptive technologies and business models that change the rules of business. The goal is to out maneuver and have a deeper understanding of the market than your competitors. It all becomes a game of probability. Like Henry Ford said, "A market is never saturated with a good product, but it is very quickly saturated with a bad."

Why International Trade?

International trade is predicated on the opportunity sought after by companies to find new markets for their products and services. In doing so most CEOs that I have spoken with tell me it is to increase their sales volume and to improve the return on investment for the company. Most are cautious about entering into unknown markets that they never had to explore before and will move slowly to learn the lay of the land. Their fear is of standing still and loosing the opportunity to someone else. For those companies that deal in seasonal products, international trade helps them to compensate for seasonal fluctuation and opens up new markets to sell their products. Executives from foreign companies that have come to the United States have told me that just by being here they have learned new and advanced business methods they can now take back to their home markets. They were enlightened to new business resources in marketing, Internet sales, product development, and a range of others that they didn't know were available to them. Most of these executives mentioned that by having established a presence in the U.S. they increased their funding opportunities not only from the contacts that they made but by their commitment to enter the U.S. knowing what was involved and the risks that they were taking.

In regione caecorum rex est luscus

The Dutch humanist, Desiderius Erasmus's observation that "In the country of the blind the one-eyed man is king" can be applied to those contemplating entry into new and unexplored markets. International trade in reality does not differ from domestic trade because the motivation of the participants is usually the same. With the Internet, enhanced communications and transportation, the deterrents for establishing international trade has greatly diminished. There are many legitimate sources of help for those contemplating establishing an international presence. Taking the time to do the required research and establishing a network of support will save you time and money in the long run. The most important prerequisite for the survival of the entrepreneurial company is to focus first on those countries where the social and cultural environment is conducive to achievement and wealth creation and the participants are held in high esteem. It also helps to have the right regulatory and tax environment that doesn't hinder those companies that take on additional risk.

Periods of great change like the one now underway force us to understand the distinctive transformation that is occurring. It is critical to understand how people of different cultures make decisions and how this will apply to pricing, manufacturing, distribution and your customer demographics.

The more connected company executives and consumers become, the more new ideas will accelerate, and innovation will be brought forth. Geographic distance will no longer matter. The key to social and business online networking is to make the community interaction worthwhile, focused, and attractive to others. The more knowledge these members contribute the more benefit there will be to the community. Web-based communities are one of the most economical ways to educate buyers and provide valuable information and counsel.

The New Silk Road

During my travels abroad I have firsthand experience of the opening of new Silk Roads that cross country boundaries and are bringing people together from around the world. At a recent trade show in Seoul, South Korea, there were buyers from China, Singapore, India, Brazil, and the European Union interested in computer electronics designed and manufactured in South Korea. The meetings that I attended were dynamic, intense, and strictly focused on doing business. Like the Silk Road of the past, international trade in this age of globalization is equally hospitable and open to new ways of conducting business. The Silk Road of today, like its predecessor, has no single route to follow and trades in many products and services. Trust, patience, and understanding still are the building blocks of trade.

Global traders have for hundreds of years been focused on the tremendous riches that could be achieved through direct trade with Asia and the New World. Christopher Columbus in 1492 sailed west to find a sea route to China. His initial disappointment was overcome when he realized the wealth potential of a "New World."

In the eighteenth century, Adam Smith observed, "China has long been one of the richest, that is, one of the most fertile, best cultivated, most industrious, and most populous countries in the world."[11]

There are those who believe that the U.S. market will become much more difficult for foreign companies to enter in the future. The consumer spending culture that typified America for the last thirty years may be shifting as individuals begin saving more and reducing their

---

11. The Wealth of Nations

spending on foreign purchases. The opportunities for foreign companies that have been prevalent in the past may not be so in the not too distant future as a result in U.S. policy shifts occurring both at the state and federal levels.

The United States has been the destination for entrepreneurs from around the world for the last five decades. It is still the primary focus for those companies looking for capital and an open market to expand and grow. What I see is that America is still and will remain for the foreseeable future the destination for these individuals and companies with vision and ambition to better themselves. Other countries are now competing for these same entrepreneurs and companies to produce tomorrow's dynamic products and to develop their markets. The relative advantage that the United States has held is gradually declining with the prevalence of off shoring, labor arbitrage, and capital outflow.

Yet for whatever may occur with the markets worldwide, I remain hopeful of the ability of the entrepreneurial spirit to rise to the occasion as it has always done in the past. The United States remains one of the most attractive countries for entrepreneurial companies because it has a deep history of risk taking and capital formation. Immigrants are at the forefront of technological innovation and entrepreneurship. Foreigners who immigrate to our shores are risk takers who in their desire for a better life start businesses and invest in America. If they fail, they pick themselves up and start again. The same way their predecessors have done in past generations. Innovation is the only way they can differentiate themselves from the others. The U.S. still offers the doorway to the world to innovative ideas and businesses.

As the American author Mark Twain said:

> "Twenty years from now you will be more disappointed by the things that you didn't do than by the ones you did do. So throw off the bowlines. Sail away from the safe harbor. Catch the trade winds in your sails. Explore. Dream. Discover."

Appendix

A Market Opportunity Online Resources[12]

---

12. Provided by Meridian Executive Resources

Trying to find your company's U.S. market potential can be a difficult task. Resources abound online regarding information about direct foreign investment, technical and service information, and channel programs. The problem is the reliability of the data. The following is a sampling of the reliable resources available to you.

Silicon Valley Resources

Asian American Manufacturing Association (AAMA): http://www.aamasv.com

American Marketing Association: http://www.svama.org

Chinese Information & Networking Association (CINA): http://www.cina.org

Chinese Software Professionals Association (CSPA): http://www.cspa.com

Garage.com: http://www.garage.com

HiTechCare: http://hitechcare.com

International Association of Business Communicators (IABC): http://www.iabc.com

Japan Society of Northern California: http://www.usajapan.org

Joint Venture Silicon Valley Network: http://www.jointventure.org

Monte Jade: http://www.montejade.org

Product Management & Development Association (PDMA): http://www.pdma.org

Progress & Freedom Foundation: http://www.pff.org

Project Management Institute (PMI): http://www.pmi.org

SRI International - Innovation Forum Series: http://www.sri.com

San Jose Business Journal: http://www.sanjose.bcentral.com

San Jose Silicon Valley Chamber of Commerce: http://www.sjchamber.com

Silicon Valley Product Management Association (SVPMA): http://svpma.tripod.com

Small Business Development Center of Silicon Valley (U.S. SBA): http://www.siliconvalley-sbdc.org

Society of Women Engineers (SWE): http://www.swe.org

Software Development Forum: http://www.sdforum.org

Stanford University - Technology Ventures Program: http://www.stanford.edu/group/stvp

The Indus Entrepreneurs: http://sv.tie.org/chapterHome/about_tie

U.S. Chamber of Commerce: http://www.uschamber.org

Women in Technology: http://www.witi.org

Palo Alto Research Center: http://www.parc.com/about/

High Technology Internet Portals, Standards, and Publications

ATM Forum: http://www.atmforum.com

Computer Telephony: http://www.computertelephony.com

Converge Digest (Voice & data convergence): http://www.convergedigest.com

Fiber Optics Online: http://www.fiberopticsonline.com

Fortune - 100 Fastest Growing U.S. Companies: http://www.fortune.com

IEEE Communications Society: http://www.comsoc.org

Internet Telephony: http://www.itmag.com

Internet Week: http://www.internetweek.com

Light Reading (Fiber optics resource center): http://www.lightreading.com

Light-Wave (Fiber Optics): http://www.light-wave.com

MPLS Forum: http://www.mplsforum.org

MIT Technology Review: http://www.technologyreview.com

Network Computing: http://www.networkcomputing.com

Optical Internetworking Forum: http://www.oiforum.com

SANS Institute (security): http://www.sans.org/

Tech Target (20 technology-specific portals): http://www.techtarget.com

Wireless Ethernet Compatibility Alliance (WECA): http://www.wi-fi.org

World of Wireless Communications: http://www.wow-com.com

Standards Bodies, Government Agencies, and Technical Associations

Armed Forces Communications & Electronics Association (AFCEA): http://www.afcea.org

Biotechnology Industry Organization (BIO): http://www.bio.org

CableLabs: http://www.cablelabs.com

Federal Communications Commission (FCC): http://www.fcc.gov

International Biometrics Industry Association (IBIA): http://www.ibia.org

IEEE: http://www.ieee.org

Internet Engineering Taskforce: http://www.ietf.org

International Telecommunications Union (ITU): http://www.itu.int

NASA Commercial Technology Network: http://www.nctn.hq.nasa.gov

National Cable & Telecommunications Association (NCTA): http://www.ncta.com

National Institute of Standards & Technology: http://www.nist.gov

Society of Cable Telecommunications Engineers (SCTE): http://www.scte.org

Storage Networking Industry Association (SNIA): http://www.snia.org

Telecommunications Industry Association (TIA): http://www.tiaonline.org

Tele-Management Forum: http://www.tmforum.org

Wall Street Technology Association (WSTA): http://www.wsta.org

Wireless Communications Alliance (WCA): http://www.wca.org

Market Research Companies

Aberdeen Group: http://www.aberdeen.com

Burton Group: http://www.burtongroup.com

Cahners In-stat Group: http://www.instat.com

Dell'Oro Group: http://www.delloro.com

eMarketer: http://www.emarketer.com

Forrester Research: http://www.forrester.com

Frost & Sullivan: http://www.frost.com

Gartner Group: http://www.gartnergroup.com

IDG: http://www.idg.com

Infonetics: http://www.infonetics.com

Jupiter Media Mix: http://www.jmm.com

Meta Group: http://www.metagroup.com

Yankee Group: http://www.yankeegroup.com

U.S. Patent & Trademark Office: http://www.uspto.gov

Venture Reporter.Net: http://www.venturereporter.net

Venture Wire: http://www.venturewire.com

Index

economic development 5, 12, 16, 23,
    158
equity financing 168, 169
equity joint ventures 114, 153
Europe 6, 11, 24, 34, 39, 43, 75, 111,
    135, 150, 154, 156, 158, 161, 162,
    181
exclusive dealers 119
express warranties 131

F

Facebook 11, 21, 46, 143, 146, 159,
    162
Falcor Wine Cellars 136
Federal Communications
    Commission 5, 107
Federal Trade Commission 108
FedEx 18
Financial Times 57, 171
Florida 41, 103
Food and Drug Administration 107
foreign direct investment 74, 76
foreign manufacturer 20, 23, 25, 43,
    118, 139, 147, 153, 154, 160, 161
France 9, 135, 177
French 9, 15, 40, 43, 161

G

GDP 22
General Douglas MacArthur 170
General Electric 81
General Mills 56
General Motors 49, 112
General suppliers 112
Geneva 70
German American Business
    Association 7
Germany 9, 161, 178, 182
global trade 9, 12, 13, 14, 18, 19, 35,
    76, 151, 182, 183, 185
globalization 7, 9, 10, 41, 60, 74, 80,
    116, 141, 146, 149, 150, 173, 175,
    178, 181, 188

Golden State Warriors 137
Google 11, 86, 111, 159, 184
Greece 9
Gucci 52

H

H&M 153
Häagen-Dazs 43
Harmonized Tariff Schedules 107
Herodotus 17
Hertzelia Pituach 15
Hewlett Packard 53
Hilo Hattie 40
Hispanic 11, 41
HiTechCare 11
Home Depot 56
Home Retail Group PLC 60
Home Shopping Network 61
Honda 139
Hong Kong 10, 15, 22, 23, 25, 34, 76,
    159
HP 144, 184

I

IBM 21, 42, 92, 111, 124
implied warranties 131
incremental sales channels 119
incubators 12, 108
India 15, 20, 23, 42, 151, 152, 156,
    157, 158, 159, 160, 161, 163, 173,
    182, 188
indirect sales 40, 104
intellectual property 13, 16, 30, 32,
    97, 100, 110, 111, 113, 115, 116,
    119, 131, 152, 157, 161
international commerce 35
International Monetary Fund 154
Internet 6, 11, 17, 21, 23, 26, 34, 40,
    41, 44, 45, 57, 58, 60, 61, 65, 67,
    68, 83, 87, 94, 110, 125, 133, 137,
    142, 143, 153, 154, 159, 162, 163,
    173, 178, 186, 187
Internet sales 40, 163, 174, 187

About the Author

Jack S. Katz is the CEO of Novusglobe LLC, an international business and market development consultancy and research company. He founded the firm after three decades of successful executive management for several well-known international corporations.

Identified as one of the ten top people to know by *Technology Decisions* magazine, Jack is noted for his knowledge and delivery of technology and business solutions that have had a dramatic impact on the bottom line of global companies. He is in frequent demand as a keynote speaker for professional and technology organizations and has delivered talks on three continents.

Jack's exceptional career began in information technology where he served in such diverse industries as retail, healthcare, financial services, and insurance. He transferred this experience to the marketing and sales sector where he advises Fortune 1000 companies both on the strategic and tactical impact of leading-edge technologies, business development, and strategic marketing. He served in executive positions at Cisco Systems, Sun Microsystems, Providian Financial Services, Blue Shield of California, and Safeway, Inc.

Jack earned a Bachelor of Arts degree and Masters of Public Administration from the University of Colorado. He has served as an adjunct faculty instructor in computer science and business administration at the University of Phoenix.

Contact:
Jack can be reached at *jack@jackkatz.com* and
http://www.jackkatz.com

Other Happy About® Books

Purchase these books at Happy About http://happyabout.info or at other online and physical bookstores.

#PARTNER tweet Book01

In a book that you can read in fifteen minutes or less, you will gain insights on smart partnering and recognize it as an asset you need to help you grow your business.

Paperback $19.95
eBook $14.95

42 Rules of Cold Calling Executives

If you are part of sales management looking to give your team something to help them with cold calling challenges or are an account rep wanting better results, this book is for you.

Paperback $19.95
eBook $14.95

42 Rules to Increase Sales Effectiveness

This book upgrades and adjusts foundational rules for today's business environment to increase individual or team overall sales effectiveness.

Paperback $19.95
eBook $14.95

I Need a Killer Press Release—Now What???

If you are a small to mid-size business owner who wants to understand online news promotion, or work for a PR firm who wants to add online optimization and SEO to your press releases, this book is written for you.

Paperback $19.95
eBook $14.95

A Message from Super Star Press™

Thank you for your purchase of this Super Star Press book. It is available online at http://happyabout.com/global-dominance.php or at other online and physical bookstores.

- Please contact us for quantity discounts at sales@happyabout.info
- If you want to be informed by email of upcoming Happy About® books, please email bookupdate@happyabout.info

Happy About is interested in you if you are an author who would like to submit a non-fiction book proposal or a corporation that would like to have a book written for you. Please contact us by email editorial@happyabout.info or phone (1-408-257-3000).

Other Happy About books available include:

- 18 Rules of Community Engagement:
  http://www.happyabout.com/community-engagement.php
- #LEADERSHIPtweet Book01:
  http://www.happyabout.com/thinkaha/leadershiptweet01.php
- #PARTNERtweet Book01:
  http://www.happyabout.com/thinkaha/partnertweet01.php
- 42 Rules for Strategic Partnerships:
  http://www.happyabout.com/42rules/strategic-partnerships.php
- 42 Rules of Cold Calling Executives:
  http://www.happyabout.com/42rules/coldcallingexecutives.php
- 42 Rules to Increase Sales Effectiveness:
  http://www.42rules.com/increase_sales_effectiveness/index.html
- 42 Rules for Driving Success With Books:
  http://www.happyabout.com/42rules/books-drive-success.php
- 42 Rules of Marketing:
  http://www.happyabout.com/42rules/marketing.php
- I Need a Killer Press Release—Now What???:
  http://www.happyabout.com/killer-press-release.php
- I'm on LinkedIn—Now What??? (Second Edition):
  http://www.happyabout.com/linkedinhelp.php
- Managing Salespeople:
  http://www.happyabout.com/managingsalespeople.php
- Red Fire Branding:
  http://www.happyabout.com/redfirebranding.php
- Social Media Success!:
  http://www.happyabout.com/social-media-success.php

Breinigsville, PA USA
25 March 2011
258424BV00002B/3/P